Your Towns and Cities in the

C000091154

Cardiff
and the Valleys
in the Great War

This book is dedicated, with the greatest respect,
to all those who serve – past, present and future.

Your Towns and Cities in the Great War

Cardiff and the Valleys in the Great War

Gary M. Dobbs

Pen & Sword
MILITARY

First published in Great Britain in 2015 by
PEN & SWORD MILITARY
an imprint of
Pen and Sword Books Ltd
47 Church Street
Barnsley
South Yorkshire S70 2AS

ISBN 978 1 78346 355 8

Printed and bound in England
by CPI Group (UK) Ltd, Croydon, CR0 4YY

Typeset in Times New Roman by Chic Graphics

Pen & Sword Books Ltd incorporates the imprints of
Pen & Sword Archaeology, Atlas, Aviation, Battleground, Discovery,
Family History, History, Maritime, Military, Naval, Politics, Railways,
Select, Social History, Transport, True Crime, Claymore Press,
Frontline Books, Leo Cooper, Praetorian Press, Remember When,
Seaforth Publishing and Wharncliffe.

For a complete list of Pen and Sword titles please contact
Pen and Sword Books Limited
47 Church Street, Barnsley, South Yorkshire, S70 2AS, England
E-mail: enquiries@pen-and-sword.co.uk
Website: www.pen-and-sword.co.uk

Contents

Acknowledgements

I am deeply in the debt of Gilly Smith for all her help regarding information about her grandfather, Herbert Paine Smith, who served with the 11th Welsh Battalion, the Cardiff Pals. In 1981 Gilly's father, Major Bob Smith, sat down with Herbert in order to record his memories of the Great War. These recordings provided me with invaluable first-hand information on the Cardiff Pals.

I also found the book, *Cardiff Pals* by K. Cooper and J.E. Davies (Militaria Cymraeg, 1988) to be a great source of information on the day-to-day life of those serving in the battalion. Thanks go too, to the staff at Cardiff Central Library – without their expertise and service this book would have been a far more difficult project. I also owe thanks to the archives of *The South Wales Echo*, *Pontypridd Observer* and *Western Mail*.

Huge thanks are due to Roni Wilkinson of Pen and Sword for holding my hand throughout this project, and Jen Newby whose careful editing greatly improved my work. Finally, I would like to acknowledge Lisa for all the help, especially in providing a never-ending supply of coffee.

Photographic Credits

Many of the photographs used throughout this book are in the public domain. However, I am grateful to *The South Wales Echo* and Media Wales for granting me permission to use images from their collections within this book.

The author took most of the war memorial photographs in Chapter Twelve.

Introduction

Looking back, with the full weight of history at our fingertips, it would seem that the First World War was inevitable. It may have taken an assassination in Sarajevo during a June afternoon in 1914 to finally tip the world over the edge and into the abyss, but for months, if not years prior to the event the dark clouds of war had been forming.

The gathering together of gigantic forces could be felt across Europe as the world approached a truly terrible period in human history. Initially known as the 'European War', the conflict would eventually draw in all of the world's great economic powers and result in shattering casualty statistics. Even today, after other terrible conflicts have been consigned to history, these statistics still seem incredible. In the end, more than 70 million military personnel were involved in what would become the biggest war in history. Nine million combatants would lose their lives, as the War employed new technology able to deliver devastation on a previously unthinkable scale.

For a world accustomed to brief, quickly resolved wars, often won and lost in a single battle, the Great War would come as a surprise. Not only would the war be fought on land and at sea, but it also took place in the air. Brutal new weapons would be used: machine guns, tanks, flamethrowers and, perhaps most terrible of all, poison gas.

By early August 1914 it was clear that Britain had no option but to enter the war. The complicated web of political allegiances across Europe meant that Britain, then Europe's greatest superpower, could not stand back while the rest of the continent imploded. Even so, only two days before Britain declared war on Germany, the British

Government and the most of the population were more inclined to remain neutral in the impending European crisis. Had Germany refrained from invading Belgium – a nation that Britain had sworn to protect in the 1839 Treaty of London – then the United Kingdom may not have become embroiled in the conflict.

A diplomatic crisis was sparked off by the assassination of Archduke Franz Ferdinand, heir to the throne of Austria-Hungry, by Yugoslav nationalist Gavrilo Princip, while the Archduke was on an official visit to Bosnia. Austria-Hungary, blaming Serbian nationalists for the murder, declared war on Serbia. In preparation for the invasion of Serbia, the Austro-Hungarians fired the first shots on 28 July 1914; this triggered a catastrophe which eventually sucked in all of the major world players.

Russia was forced into the crisis because it had sworn to protect Serbia. This led Germany, then aligned with Austria, to issue a warning that if Russia came out in defence of Serbia, the German Government would, in turn, declare war on Russia. During this period Germany was a relatively new country on the world stage, having only recently been formed by the amalgamation of the Prussian states, and the thought of being surrounded by warring nations terrified the German Government.

When the British ultimatum regarding Belgium was ignored by the Germans, Britain declared war on Germany at midnight on 4 August 1914. In the meantime the German invasion of neutral Belgium and Luxembourg spread into France. After the Allied Forces eventually halted the German advance on Paris, a stalemate was quickly reached and a static front line known as the Western Front opened up. The war in Europe became a war of attrition, with a front line that would change very little until 1917.

While trench warfare has provided the most abiding images of the Great War, along with the phrase, 'Over the top', this is a restricted view of the conflict. Today we might imagine a war measured in yards of mud along a small area of France, when, in reality, theatres of war also opened up in Italy, Africa, Asia and Turkey. An exclusive focus on the Western Front also ignores the war that was being fought at sea and, for the first time, in the air. The War was fought in many different ways too; not only in the various theatres of war were sacrifices being made and great bravery displayed. In a sense, this war was also fought on the Home Front and those who stayed in Britain faced struggles that were significant, if not comparable with those endured by soldiers on the battlefield.

On the outbreak of war Cardiff was one of the richest trading centres in the world, and had recently been granted city status in 1905. The city's wealth came from the coal – often referred to as 'black gold' – mined in its surrounding valleys, which was exported around the world. It was in Cardiff, at the Coal Exchange on Mount Stuart Square, that Britain's first million pound deal was struck in 1907.

In August 1914, it was evident that the mining industry in Cardiff and throughout the rest of Britain would be of vital importance to the War Effort. During the conflict the price of coal rose at a staggering rate and, although a large proportion of their workforce disappeared into the various sections of the armed services, the coal magnates did not suffer financially from the conflict. The Government swiftly pushed new laws through Parliament to ensure that a reliable workforce was maintained within the mines, as well as in many other essential industries.

The people of Cardiff were initially excited by the War and eager to do their bit in any way they could, like those in most towns and cities throughout Britain. Mothers proudly waved off sons who had taken the King's shilling; wives boasted of spouses fighting for King and Country; young men dreamt of putting on a military uniform and defending their homeland. In 1914 Britain was a self-confident, powerful nation, and the British people felt they belonged to a prime force on the world stage. Britain also held the biggest overseas empire in history at that time and in consequence dominated world trade. The general assumption was that now Britain had joined the conflict, the Allied Forces would achieve a quick and decisive victory.

Yet, in 1914 the British Army was tiny in comparison to the armies of the other major European powers. On the outbreak of war, the British Army boasted 975,000 men including reservists – a figure

Kaiser Wilhelm II apparently regarded with contempt in comparison with his own army of some 4,500,000. The lack of manpower and the fact that many seasoned soldiers were serving in far-flung corners of the British Empire meant that thousands of volunteers, as well as Reservists and Territorials would be required to fill the ranks of the British Army.

Alongside every town, city, hamlet and village in the United Kingdom, Cardiff and the surrounding area subsequently sent forth large numbers of men to war. The following chapters of this book tell the story not only of the War itself, but of the ways in which it affected those far from the battlefields and how a nation stood together in the face of a seemingly all-conquering force.

CHAPTER 1

1914 – A Call to Arms

Timeline of key events in 1914

June

28   Assassination of Archduke Ferdinand

July

23   Austria-Hungary sends an ultimatum to Serbia
28   Austria-Hungary declares war on Serbia

August

3   Germany declares war on France
4   Great Britain declares war on Germany
7   The British Expeditionary Force arrives in France
12   Great Britain declares war on Austria-Hungary
14   The Battle of the Frontiers begins
23   The Battle of Mons
26   The Battle of Le Cateau
28   The Battle of Heligoland Bight
30   Amiens captured by German troops

September

5   Retreat from Mons by Allied forces
6   The Battle of the Marne
12   The Battle of Aisne
13   The Battle of the Marne ends

October

4   The Royal Naval Division arrives at Antwerp

10   Antwerp surrenders to the Germans

19   The First Battle of Ypres begins

November

1   Allied forces commences hostilities against Turkey
    The Allies invade German East Africa

2   The Allied blockade of Germany begins

3   Dardanelles forts are bombarded by the Allied Fleet
    The Battle of Tanga begins in German East Africa

6   Allied operations at Basra commenced

7   British and Japanese forces capture the German-controlled
    port of Tsingtao

9   The Battle of Cocos

December

8   The Battle of the Falklands

16   German warships bombard the British East Coast

25   The Christmas Truce

Although Britain did not declare war on Germany until midnight on 4 August 1914, preparations for war started twenty-four hours earlier in Cardiff. On 3 August, sailors from all over South Wales answered calls to report to navel bases. In total sixty men were called up from Cardiff, and the city's General Station was packed with relatives and friends who had come to wave them off on what was then seen as a great adventure. The station became so packed that the gates had to be closed and the police called in to control the crowds.

The South Wales Echo reported that the crowds sang patriotic songs with great gusto as they bid the men farewell. The Salvation Army band from Grangetown had escorted one of their members, a naval reservist, to the station and its members sang hymns as the men boarded the trains that would take them on the first part of their journey towards war. At 11.30pm, minutes before the deadline for the German

Government's response expired, the trains pulled out of Cardiff and there was an enthusiastic roar from the gathered crowds. Half-an-hour later Britain was officially at war.

This scene would be replayed day after day, as more and more reservists reported for duty and the streets filled with servicemen in uniform. Many of these men had a girl on each arm, reported the *South Wales Echo*, in an article discussing the glamour of the military uniform. In pubs across the city soldiers and sailors were treated to free drinks and civilians looked on them with respect and pride.

For years many people had believed that sooner or later Britain would have to fight Germany, and now the anticipated conflict had happened, claimed the *Pontypridd Observer* on 5 August 1914. 'No wise man wants war,' the paper's editorial asserted, 'but as we have to fight, let us fight as one man with the sole aim and determination to come out on top. We must win, we will win. There is no doubt about that.'

Only hours before war was officially declared, the *South Wales Echo* had carried the following story, under the headline 'British Ultimatum to Germany':

> In the House of Commons this afternoon Mr Asquith, the Prime Minister, said a telegram had been sent to the British Ambassador at Berlin. The telegram informed the British Ambassador of the appeal made by the King of the Belgians for diplomatic intervention. Belgium had categorically refused to sanction the flagrant violation of the Law of Nations involved in the threat by Germany.
>
> The German government has been asked to give a satisfactory reply, by midnight, on the question of Belgium neutrality.

The declaration placed the country in a state of nervous excitement,with some people expecting imminent attack. The same edition of the newspaper also carried the story of a dramatic engagement between the British and German Fleets in the North Sea, and claimed that nine German warships had been sunk, as well as one British dreadnought. A similar report printed by local newspapers in the Newcastle area, asserted that two British cargo boats close to the firing line had come into the Tyne carrying many injured men.

These stories were unconfirmed and, although they were later proven false, at the time the rumours were given sufficient credence for Newcastle Hospital to be put on standby to receive the wounded. It later emerged that naval manoeuvres had been carried out in the North Sea a week before war was declared, during an incident which had involved the firing of live shells.

Immediately following the declaration of war, four German ships docked in Cardiff were seized, with their cargos impounded and crews imprisoned. During this period there were around 35,000 Germans living in Britain. Many returned home on the outbreak of war, but of those who remained some found themselves interned in camps under the new Aliens Registration Act. A considerable proportion of male internees had British wives and sweethearts, and these women faced mounting prejudice as the war escalated.

Spurred on by the atmosphere of excitement and rumour, men all over the United Kingdom were eager to get into uniform and serve their country in a skirmish that most believed would be over by Christmas. 'We the young were very patriotic when the 1914 war broke out and the first thing we wanted to do was join up,' recalled Herbert Paine Smith, who served in the 11th Battalion, Welsh Regiment. There was a mood of intense patriotism across the country and thousands of men enlisted, hoping to reach the Front before the fighting ended. Wales was no different, despite the protests of non-conformist preachers who felt that the Welsh should remain aloof from the war.

Many of these men responded to Lord Kitchener's ongoing call throughout the autumn of 1914. Appointed Secretary of State for War by the British Government, Kitchener was in charge of raising what he termed a 'New Army' of 100,000 volunteers; by the end of the year more than a million had enlisted. Lord Kitchener was one of the few Government figures to anticipate that the War would last for several years, and he immediately put himself at odds with the Cabinet when he stated that the War would continue for at least three years and require a massive new army. At the time Britain was the only major European power not to have a conscription system in place and Kitchener urged for a nationwide appeal for volunteer soldiers to be made. He also warned that there would be a tremendous number of casualties before the war was over, famously predicting that the outcome of the war would be decided by the last million men Britain could throw into battle. This sobering forecast was largely ignored and the belief that the war would be over by Christmas continued to persist.

Kitchener's New Army was intended to provide the armed forces with extra strength and, in what was considered a revolutionary move, men from the same town or workplace were allowed to enlist and serve together in Pals Battalions. The fact that they could train

Herbert Kitchener, 1st Earl Kitchener.

and serve together with men they had known for years was tremendously appealing for many recruits. The possibility that they might also die together, with a single battle instantly depleting the male population of a particular area, was conveniently overlooked.

In Cardiff there was a rush to join the 11th Battalion of the Welsh Regiment (later known as the Cardiff Pals). The city's Maindy Barracks processed so many volunteers that extra staff had to be laid on and the police called in to keep the large crowds under control. Coal miners, businessmen, policemen, teachers, and dentists – men from all walks of life enlisted. They were friends and colleagues who drank in the same pubs, played on the same soccer and rugby fields and, in some cases, had attended school together.

Many of the new recruits were concerned that the fighting would end before they were trained. Yet the War would not end by Christmas 1914. After two further Christmases had come and gone the *Pontypridd Observer* published a 'war alphabet' in January 1917. The author, although uncredited, was very likely a staff reporter tasked with writing moral-boosting editorial.

Recruits to the 11th Battalion of the Welsh Regiment, or the Cardiff Pals.

A for the army we join when we're fit.
B for the Boshes we're determined to hit.
C for the Canadians – courageous and strong.
D the Dominion to which they belong.
E stands for Emden, elusive destroyer.
F the fatigue we suffered to decoy her.
G for the Guns which such havoc create.
H for the Huns and their hymn of fate.
I stands for India, loyal and true.
J for the jealousy such possessions imbue.
K of course Kitchener silent and stern.
L for the lessons he would have us learn.
M for Marines as busy as bees.
N for the Navy which keeps free the seas.
O stands for Ocean, deep, rolling and wide.
P for the piracy the Huns wish to hide.
Q is the quarrel the Germans affected.
R the result they never expected.
S for Salonika where the Allies have landed.
T for the Turks who will soon be disbanded.

U for Ultimatums sent out galore.
V for the Victims of this terrible war.
W for Wilhelm full of rage and despair.
X – pecting [sic] *to meet with his death in the air.*
Y for the Youths who have sacrificed all.
Z for the Zeppelins lost in the squall.

In 1914 it was not anticipated that there would be much enthusiasm to enlist among the young Welsh male population. Welshmen had displayed an historical ambivalence to the British Army. In the past the lack of recruits from Wales had meant English soldiers filled the ranks of the Royal Welch Fusiliers, who were often called the 'Birmingham Fusiliers' for good reason. Welsh Non-Conformism and Liberalism were powerful anti-establishment forces, combined with an inbuilt hostility towards militarism. This, along with the working class militancy evidenced in many of the recent pre-war Welsh mining strikes, suggested that the war fever affecting the rest of the United Kingdom might not spread to Wales.

However, a fierce tide of support for the war swept Wales. Over 280,000 Welshmen served during 1914–1918 and around 35,000 were killed. On the morning following the outbreak of war, the editorial of the *Western Mail* urged readers to enlist: 'Let it not be recorded to our eternal shame that young Welsh men were playing cricket and football while the nation's call for soldiers continued unfulfilled.'

In September 1914 the *South Wales Echo* reported on the re-enlistment of sixty-six-year-old, Welshman Sergeant Alfred Bickenton, who would act as an instructor for new troops. He was re-enlisted by Colour Sergeant Owen, who had himself been recruited by Bickenton many years previously. Although Alfred Bickenton had originally joined the army in 1864, according to the newspaper he was 'as fit as a fiddle', having passed his medical 'with flying colours'. It was also deemed newsworthy that a local 'coloured man' had enlisted and was to serve in the Army Service Corps.

There was much excitement in Cardiff when 120 wounded soldiers returned from the Front and arrived in the city for hospital treatment on Sunday, 13 September 1914. They were soon receiving visitors and reunited with their families. Many of them were interviewed by the local newspapers and modestly narrated their experiences, passing over the hardships of the Front and praising the bravery of the officers who had led them. The men were also visited by Sir William James Thomas, Knight of Ynyshir, who was anxious to ensure that everything possible was done for the soldiers' comfort and well-being. Born in Caerphilly, Thomas was a colliery owner and philanthropist renowned for donating money to medical facilities. His charitable work had gained him a knighthood earlier in the year.

Throughout September 1914, the recruitment continued apace and on 15 September, *The South Wales Echo* published a statement from a Major Lucus, the staff recruiting officer at the central recruiting station based in Gladstone School on Whitchurch Road. It noted that 6,250 men had joined up so far, and that there were still many more recruits to process. A record was also set in Pontypridd, the valleys town several miles north of Cardiff, when 100 men were recruited in a single day. Most of these men, nicknamed 'Ponty's Finest', would serve with the Shropshire Light Infantry and the Lancashire Fusiliers, joining the 600 men from the district who had volunteered during the previous ten days.

The influx of new recruits poured in so swiftly that a few days later the War Office announced the closure of recruitment for several regiments, including: the Royal Engineers, the Royal Horse Artillery, the Royal Welch Fusiliers, the Welsh Regiment, the Cheshire Regiment, the South Wales Borderers and the Suffolk Regiment.

Meanwhile, the rush to join up continued. In the town of Bridgend scores of young miners from the valley attended the drill hall in order to join Kitchener's 'New Army', and over 100 recruits were passed by the doctors. As the numbers mounted, it was soon necessary to delay the deployment of new recruits to the various depots and many found themselves being sent home to wait until they could be called up.

In Cardiff, several players from Cardiff City Football Club registered their names for immediate active service, following a decision by the club to cancel all forthcoming fixtures for the 1914/1915 season. Although the league was restarted the following year, the team was much diminished and most of their wartime fixtures were friendly matches, with players allowed time off from the army to take part whenever possible. Two Cardiff players, Tom Witts and Wally Stewart, lost their lives in action, while Jack Evans, the first player to sign as a professional with the club, was in Germany with the victorious British Army in 1918.

Local football hero Fred Keenor, who would captain the Cardiff team in their 1927 FA Cup victory against Arsenal, was wounded at the Battle of the Somme in 1916. His injuries threatened to end his footballing career, but through determination he recovered and went on to play for a number of years, remaining with Cardiff City until 1931. He then played for Crewe Alexandra, and, even after quitting professional football in 1934, he continued to play with non-league teams for several years.

Eventually, sportsmen's battalions were set up, along the same lines as the Pals Battalions. The most famous was the 17th Middlesex Battalion, fondly known as the 'Football Battalion', which numbered Cardiff City's Fred Keenor within its recruits.

All recruits had to meet certain official standards to enlist: a height of over 5ft 3in, a chest measurement of at least 34in, and to be aged between nineteen and thirty-five. However, recruiting sergeants were not all equally scrupulous and, particularly later on in the War, very little evidence of age was required. Fred Cox, a sixteen-year-old butcher's errand boy from Penarth Road, Cardiff was told by a recruiting officer that he would need to supply a note from his parents to prove he was of age. A resourceful young man, Fred asked a friend to write the note and he was promptly enlisted.

The fitness standards were also flouted, as in the case of Evan Lewis Morgan, a twenty-one-year-old miner from the Welsh Navigation Pit at Coedely. Morgan had a lazy eye, which he could not focus, but he managed to pass the visual test by peeping through his fingers at the card on the wall. Recruiting sergeants initially earned two shillings and sixpence for every man they signed up (this was later reduced to one shilling), and the doctors examining the men were paid a similar amount for each man they passed as fit.

Fred Keenor, surrounded by Cardiff City players, holds the FA Cup 1927.

Cardiff City FC 1913/1914.

The sudden influx of new soldiers caused a nightmare for those within the military who were responsible for co-ordinating recruits. New soldiers would often arrive at an army barracks only to find that no uniforms or weapons had been provided for them, and they would begin their basic training wearing civvies. In his 1919 book, *For Remembrance: An account of some fateful years*, Harry Cartmell describes an incident in September 1914, when over 200 Welsh miners who had been sent to a Preston training camp suddenly appeared at Preston Railway Station carrying banners which read 'No Food, no Shelter, no Money'. These men had left their jobs and families behind and now, after two weeks away from home, they had had enough and demanded to be put on a train back home to South Wales.

The mayor was summoned and he learned that the Welshmen's service to their country had thus far consisted of wandering around in the rain with no money in their pockets, as none of the recruits had received a penny of their army pay. This small-scale mutiny was resolved when the miners were pacified by a lavish meal at Preston Town Hall. Like thousands of others, after initial delays they were eventually kitted out, given army accommodation and paid.

Any illusions Britons had about what the war would be like were shattered within the first few weeks of the conflict. By September 1914 the newspapers were filled with horrific reports of events at the Front Line. The Battle of Mons, which began on 23 August, was the first major battle of the War with significant British involvement, and on 6 September the *South Wales Echo* relayed the sombre news that after nine days of fighting there had been around 15,000 British casualties. The *Echo* also stated that in the days following the Battle of Mons, 'there had been a period of fighting that had been continuous and deadly'. The same edition noted the loss of HMS *Pathfinder*, a British cruiser which had struck a mine some 20 miles out to sea. Of the 270 men on board, the ship's captain and between fifty to sixty men had been saved.

It was announced that the bells of parish churches throughout South Wales would be rung for five minutes at noon each day, as a call to pray for the soldiers and sailors now engaged in the war.

British Forces gathered at Mons.

The South Wales Daily News ran an article on 5 September stating that fifteen British fishing boats had been sunk in the North Sea and many of their crew members captured. Panic had also spread across Britain on the previous day, when an airship had been spotted over an airfield in Woolwich, south-east London. The airship, described as grey in colour, was flying high and in a westerly direction towards London, however it was eventually identified as a Royal Naval airship.

As the casualties increased and the months passed, most people knew at least one serviceman who had been killed or injured in battle. Yet, the rush to enlist in the armed forces continued apace. Men who failed the fitness test would return home and start exercising, lifting weights and running, hoping to make a more successful second attempt.

Support for the war was bolstered by the arrival of Belgian refugees

Belgian Refuges arrive at Rhyl and are welcomed by large crowds.

in Britain, bringing with them stories of the German invasion. These tales were repeated and often exaggerated in public houses and newspapers, rapidly travelling across the country. Over a quarter of a million Belgians came into the United Kingdom during September 1914 alone, and many were billeted with families in Cardiff and the outlying valleys. This remains the biggest ever intake of refugees in British history – a fact that is largely forgotten today. Although the majority of the Belgians returned home after the War, many chose to stay in their new homes and their descendants remain in the country today. It was estimated at the start of 1915 that Wales had accommodated around 1,000 Belgian refugees.

Despite refugees, scare stories, and the departure of hundreds of young men, the people of Cardiff got on with their lives. The War was always at the back of their minds, however, and often its effects were all too visible. Those at home were also determined to contribute to the War Effort. Local women, many of them wives and mothers of men serving in the conflict, began fundraising by any means open to them, and soon door to door collections, jumble sales and concerts were springing up throughout the local area. It would become increasingly clear as the conflict progressed that this truly was the people's war.

CHAPTER 2

Pals – The March to War

...keep thy friend.
Under thy own life's key

(William Shakespeare, Act I, Scene I,
All's Well That Ends Well)

The 'Pride of Cardiff' went to war one sunny September morning in 1914, according to J.E. Davies and Ken Cooper in *The Cardiff Pals*. Davies's father had served with C Company in the 11th Battalion, the Welsh Regiment, having enlisted at the tender age of fifteen. He, like many other young men, considered it an honour to serve in one of the newly formed Pals Battalions.

On 14 September 1914, the Cardiff Pals Commercial Battalion (the 11th Welsh) marched from Maindy Barracks to Cardiff General Station. The Pals' initial destination was to be a training camp in the Sussex market town of Lewes. Where they might go from there remained a secret, though the prevailing feeling was that they were unlikely to see much action before the War was over.

All along the route they were cheered by the vast crowds gathered. The pavements and roads were filled with people waving and cheering, as the newly enlisted men strode forward. The soldiers moved down Whitchurch Road in neat columns of four, carrying suitcases and hold-alls. At one point in their journey, a Cathays shopkeeper ran out of his shop and thrust a loaf of bread into a soldier's hands. Mothers and sweethearts ran along the pavements, waving at their men. Many of these men would never return to Cardiff again, and of those who did a large number would be disabled; all would be irrefutably changed by their experiences.

As the men marched, some would discreetly fall out if they spotted a pretty girl in the crowd, taking a last opportunity to pass a note or make a date, before catching up with the columns. Sergeant Fred Williams found that someone had slipped a note into his haversack. It read: 'My name is Maud. I'm 19 and live at 57 De Beauvoir, Hackney Road, London. Why don't you write to me, whoever you are.' Fred wrote to Maud throughout the War, and when he returned home they married and settled in Llandaff.

Today was a special day and the men were given a worthy send-off as they marched down Whitchurch Road towards the city centre besides their brothers, friends and workmates. These were ordinary men and, had the War not intervened, they would have simply got on with their lives. Now they felt like heroes who had answered the call of their King and would soon be fighting for every man, woman and child in the cheering crowds.

The idea behind the Pals Battalions was that if men from the same area or workplace were allowed to serve together then strong relationships forged in civilian life would be carried over into military service. All over the country Pals Battalions were formed from groups of men who worked in the same industries, played particular sports, or attended public schools. Most consisted of men who had lived in the same town, perhaps growing up only streets apart. David Lloyd George, who would become Prime Minister in 1916, wanted to combine the Welsh battalions to form an entirely Welsh army, but this idea was quashed by Kitchener who believed that, whilst a Welsh division was acceptable, an entire Welsh army might prove unreliable.

However, the flaw in the concept of the Pals Battalions would become only too apparent as the War dragged on, and towns and villages lost a large proportion of their young men during single battles. Such was the case with the Cardiff Pals, who served in both France and Salonika until the Battalion was virtually wiped out within a few

Cardiff Pals marching to the railway station.

hours on a single morning in September 1918. The Macedonian battles are often overlooked in histories of the First World War, but this theatre was just as deadly as the Western Front, and often more so. Just like the men in Flanders, they could be blown apart by an enemy shell, shot down by machine gun fire or gassed, but they also endured the constant threat of disease. Out in the highlands of Macedonia malaria, dysentery, sunstroke and later Spanish influenza were often deadly.

Summer 1914: New recruits
It would be a long road for the Cardiff Pals from bidding their city farewell to fighting for their lives in Macedonia four years later. The summer of 1914 had been a rare scorcher and as September rolled around there was little sign of the winter to come; the young men who headed to the various recruiting stations around Cardiff were in high spirits as they took the King's shilling. On the way to the recruiting offices they would have seen the various sandwich-board men walking through the city, emblazoned with messages calling on local men to join up, to give their all for King and Country and avoid being called shirkers.

Oswald Sturdy, a teacher from Eleanor Street School in Bute Town, was among the many who signed up early in September 1914. He was dismayed to find that there were no uniforms waiting for the recruits, but soon mollified when he was presented with a regimental badge, which he promptly pinned to the lapel of his suit. For several weeks the badge would be the only piece of official uniform that Oswald and his fellow recruits would possess. The response to Kitchener's call for 100,000 men had overwhelmed the army supply department.

Oswald Sturdy had joined up with another teacher from the same school, James (Jimmy) Griffiths, and they were both placed in No 4 Platoon, A Company. Soon, platoon after platoon was filled, each one with men who had worked together in civilian life. No 4 Platoon alone contained employees of the Howells department store, the Cardiff Gas Company and several firms of solicitors. No 2 Platoon of A Company had a Jewish section, which was made up of businessmen like the Fligelstone brothers. Together with Jewish soldiers from other platoons, these men all lined up one morning to hand back the bacon they had been served for breakfast.

Eventually, so many men joined the Welsh Regiment that it expanded to 34 battalions. Firms such as Howells were proud that members of their workforce had joined up, and some promised to re-employ these men once the War was over – a policy that was praised in newspapers of the day. A meeting of the Cardiff Chamber of Commerce passed a resolution on 7 September 1914 that men who had left their jobs to serve should be reinstated in their old positions in peacetime as a matter of course. That same evening, 40 men from the Howells store threw in their lot with the Cardiff Pals. Around this time most of the Cardiff Corinthians soccer team also enlisted, including the skipper Jim Boswell. The team had won the Welsh Amateur League that year, beating Holywell 1 – 0 at Newton.

In October, Prime Minister Asquith arrived in Cardiff as part of his nationwide tour and spoke at a rally held in the Park Hall. His rousing speech ended with the following words:

> Men of Wales, leave to your children the richest of all inheritances – the memory of fathers who in a great cause put self sacrifice before ease, and honour before life itself.

The Prime Minister was preaching to the converted, as the first batch of the Cardiff Pals were already at army training camps, now properly kitted out and eager to see action. Yet it took almost a year from their enlistment until the first Cardiff Pals were finally ready for war. On 4 September 1915, the 11th Battalion, the Cardiff Pals, sailed from Southampton towards their destination on the Somme. The Pals were aware of what was happening over in France and knew that two battalions of the Welsh Regiment had already gone into the lines and been badly mauled.

The 2nd Welsh had lost 220 men at the Battle of Aisne. The remainder of the battalion had then taken part in the First Battle of Ypres, during which 203 men were killed, including Lieutenant Colonel C.B. Morland. Another 416 men were wounded. The 2nd Welsh had been heavily reinforced after this and subsequently lost 65 men, with 102 wounded in the Battle of Givenchy. Soon after, the Second Battle of Ypres, another 206 men fell.

The Pals would have known of these figures when they boarded the ships at Southampton. With some time to wait before the ships were ready to sail, the men took the opportunity to write to their parents, wives and sweethearts back in South Wales. For many these would be the last letters they would ever write. Private Herbert Paine Smith and Private Bjarne Nilson, whose close friendship had led to them receiving the nickname 'Heavenly Twins', spent almost the entire voyage playing card games like Brag and Nap. Several other men joined them and IOUs were played for.

Lance Corporal Johnson.

Upon arrival in France the Pals found themselves billeted in the town of Suzanne, where they were attached to the 1st Devonshire Regiment for trench duty instruction. On 9 September, the Pals took over a section of the line from the 43rd French Regiment. Twelve days later, on 21 September, the first of the Pals died on active service when a German shell hit his dug-out. This was twenty-four-year-old Lance-Corporal Alfred Johnson. His comrades had little time to reflect on their loss; in wartime there was always a job to be done.

Many of the Pals would soon become hardened by the life they led in the trenches. Former Cardiff schoolteacher, Sergeant Jimmy Griffiths wrote in his diary:

> The order comes to get some sleep. Where in them 'oles cut out of the back wall of the trenches. Sodden sacking and leaky bits of corrugated iron. Utter exhaustion brings sleep – and the lice take possession for the duration. The night has its nightmares of horror. Large screeching rats possess the living and scamper over all, devouring and terrifying where they will. And the heavy, pervading stench of death remains, a trinity with the rats and lice.

The men had been warned of the prevalence of lice in the trenches when they joined up. Seasoned men often remarked that new recruits wouldn't be proper soldiers until they had felt lice crawling over their skin. But the rats were something else, and many of the men found themselves unable to sleep for fear of the creatures, until fatigue finally overcame them.

On 7 October 1915, the 11th Welsh were relieved by the 7th South Wales Borderers and found themselves pulled from the Front Line and billeted at Framerville. Two days later, however, a second Pal was killed, this time behind the lines. Twenty-four-year-old Private Billy Coutts was accidentally shot while training on a Lewis gun. Soon after, the Pals lost a third man when twenty-one-year-old Emlyn Pryce-Matthews was shot through the head by a German sniper. Shortly before this incident, Pryce-Matthews had told a fellow soldier that he thought they should not regard the Germans as beasts, and that he felt they were simply patriots doing their duty. The following day, Captain Sanders of A Company was shot in the head by a sniper; he was the last Pal to be killed in France.

The stalemate between the British and Germans continued. In some places the Allied and German lines were so close that soldiers in each trench were able to shout to each other, which they often did, hurling insults and threats back and forth. In *Cardiff Pals*, K. Cooper and J.E.

Davies recount an anecdote in which a Private, then crouching in his trench, shouted out to the nearby German trench, "What about your flaming Navy then." (This was a reference to rumours before the Battle of Jutland that German ships had been hiding in port.) A reply was returned in perfect English: "Will you please take three bottles of larger for one of Scotch whisky?" How the Germans had known that the Pals had whisky, they never discovered, but the Private, knowing that whisky was hard to come by at the Front, answered, "Make it twelve bottles and we'll consider it."

Gradually, the Cardiff Pals realised that what had seemed a great adventure when they started out at Maindy Barracks a little over twelve months ago had now become a dangerous and uncomfortable existence. The Battalion was stationed miles behind the line and often billeted in old barns or any structure with a roof, but the men apparently refused to allow their spirits to drop and, for the most part, managed to put on a brave face.

In command of the Cardiff Pals was Colonel H. Russell Parkinson, affectionately referred to by his men as 'Parkie'. He could be firm, but was known to be fair and treated the men under his command with respect. Under Parkinson's command, the Cardiff Pals remained in France until October 1915, when the order came through that the Battalion was being sent to Salonika to fight the Bulgars (Bulgarian forces). The general reaction was one of relief: if they were going to fight then it would be better to do so in a warmer and more comfortable climate. However, there was disappointment when it was revealed that their beloved Colonel would not be coming with them. The man who had trained the Pals, transformed them from happy-go-lucky civilians into a formidable fighting unit now had to pass his troops

Colonel H. Russell Parkinson, proud commander of the Cardiff Pals until October 1915.

on to a new commanding officer, as the top brass considered Parkie too old for the rigours of the Macedonian climate.

On 28 October 1915, Colonel H. Russell Parkinson handed over command of the 11th Welsh to Colonel Victor Cowley of the 9th Royal Lancashires, who had been a prison governor in civilian life. He believed in iron discipline and, although the men initially resented his brutal ways, they had to put up with Cowley and accept this treatment as part of their lot. As the men boarded the ship with their new commanding officer, each in turn paused at the gangplank and shook hands with Colonel Parkinson, who became tearful at the sight of his men setting off for Salonika without him.

The Pals sailed on the White Star liner RMS *Megantic* during the eleven-day voyage across submarine infested seas, where at any moment an unseen torpedo might come hurtling through the depths. Every day Cowley would take them through their ship drill, shouting down any man he thought too slow or clumsy, and allowing no one to rest until they had performed to his satisfaction. This continued until 8 November, when twenty-six officers and 841 other ranks disembarked at Salonika with no clear idea of what lay ahead.

The Cardiff Pals travelled to Salonika in 1915 on board RMS Megantic, *pictured here*

CHAPTER 3

1915 – A Grim Realisation

Timeline of key events in 1915

January

15　The War Council authorises a naval attack on the Dardanelles

19　The First Zeppelin raid on Great Britain takes place at Great Yarmouth

24　Battle of Dogger Bank between Royal Navy and the German Navy

26　Defence of the Suez Canal begins

February

4　Germany declares the waters surrounding Great Britain a war zone

March

10　Battle of Neuve Chapelle begins

14　Light cruiser *Dresden*, the last German cruiser left at sea, is sunk by the British

15　The first aircraft attack is carried out on a British merchant vessel, the SS *Blonde*

28　SS *Falaba* becomes the first British passenger ship to be sunk by a German submarine

April

17   Hill 60 near Ypres is captured by the British
22   The Second Battle of Ypres begins. The battle sees the first use of chlorine gas
24   The Battle of St Julien begins
25   Allied landings at Gallipoli
26   A treaty with the Triple Entente brings Italy into the War on the side of the Allies

May

1   The Battle of St Julien ends
7   RMS *Lusitania* is sunk by a German U-boat
9   The leading division of the British New Army sails for France
25   The Second Battle of Ypres ends
31   First Zeppelin raid on London

June

5   British and French ministers attend the first conference to coordinate war policy, in Calais
7   A German airship (L.37) is attacked successfully by Royal Flying Corps fighter

July

2   The British Government creates the Ministry of Munitions
9   German forces surrender in South-West Africa
11   SMS *Konigsberg* is scuttled
15   The National Registration Act becomes law in Great Britain, requiring all eligible men to register for armed service

August

12   First sinking of an enemy ship by a torpedo dropped from a British plane
16   The small mining village of Lowca is shelled by a German submarine, which had slipped into the Solway Firth to target the Workington Iron and Steel Company

September

25   The Battle of Loos begins, during which the British Army
        use poison gas for the first time
30   Lord Derby assumes control of military recruitment in
        Britain

October

3   Allied troops land at Salonika
8   The Battle of Loos ends
12   Nurse Edith Cavell is executed in Brussels by order of a
        German court martial, after she is convicted of aiding
        around 200 Allied soldiers to escape German-occupied
        Belgium

November

11   The British advance on Baghdad begins

December

7   Ottoman forces begin their siege of the British-held town of
        Kut, near Baghdad
19   Douglas Haig succeeds Sir John French as commander of
        the British Expeditionary Force
20   The Allied evacuation of Anzac Cove is completed
25   Second Christmas truce
28   Evacuation of the Gallipoli Peninsula ordered

As 1915 approached, the war widely predicted to end by Christmas
continued to rage. When the New Year came and went without any
prospect of peace, people realised that this would not be the swiftly
concluded conflict they had expected but something else entirely. This
grim realisation only made those left at home all the more determined
to do everything within their power to help in the War Effort, and a
sense of unity was felt as people from all walks of life came together
for a common cause.

Members of the Grangetown Women's War Club meet to discuss ways to contribute to the War Effort.

On 7 January 1915, *The Western Mail* ran an article examining the review of the War that Lord Kitchener had delivered in the House of Lords the previous night. The Allies, Kitchener remarked, had made considerable progress at various points during the last couple of months, and he made much of the Austrian retreat in the Carpathians in which the Allies had taken 50,000 prisoners of war. He also commented that the recent Serbian successes against the Austrians and the Russian victory in Caucasus could have a far reaching influence upon German-led Turkish operations in the East.

Whilst there had been a drop in the numbers of men enlisting over the Christmas period, Kitchener had emphasised that the situation was improving, and 218,000 men had recently joined up. In conclusion, he argued that the problems experienced by the British authorities during the early days of the War were over: there were now sufficient numbers of officers to train new men and plentiful supplies, with a uniform ready for every recruit.

The War Effort in Cardiff

While the city's young men flocked to join the Pals, on the Home Front Cardiff's civilians were also eager to do their bit. On 8 January 1915 the Lady Mayoress of Cardiff attended the first meeting of the Grangetown Women's War Club, officially opening the club and wishing the members well in their future endeavours to aid the War Effort. This was just one among many such organisations set up across the country to raise funds to send supplies to the troops. In addition to clubs and groups, another popular means of fundraising was through concerts, often called 'smoking concerts' because their profits would be used to send cigarettes and tobacco to the troops at the Front. These concerts were particularly popular in the Welsh Valleys. The town of Pontypridd hosted many lavish smoking concerts which men, women and children from all over the local area would attend in order to contribute to the War Effort and have a good time in the process.

On Tuesday, 12 January 1915, a concert was held at the Bonvilston Hotel in Trallwn, Pontypridd, with the proceeds devoted to purchasing tobacco and cigarettes for soldiers from the ward who were now serving at the Front. Councillor T. Taylor presided over the concert and made the following speech:

> It is encouraging to find so many young men volunteering to fight the country's battles. Today the war news has been very encouraging and I hope this trend continues. I am anxious to see our Navy join the fray, because we have the most powerful ships in the world and I have every confidence that once they get at the enemy they will sink their ships. We have wounded servicemen here tonight including Private G. Beazer who has been wounded by shrapnel in his left calf and right knee. At the Battle of Aisne he won the Distinguished Conduct Medal for

saving the life of a Lieutenant. He also saw action in the battles at Mons and Ypres and I'm sure he has made all the Trallwn boys very proud of him.

(Pontypridd Observer, 14 January 1915)

The Councillor went on to mention several other serving soldiers from the area in his speech, and then the show began. Comedy skits were acted out, patriotic songs were sung, and dance routines were performed up for the ecstatic audience.

In addition to these concerts, money was raised for the War Effort through a multitude of methods. Door-to-door collections were arranged, jumble sales were held, and civilians went about these tasks with the same fervour displayed by the young men rushing to enlist. The Mayor of Llanelli made a plea in the *Western Mail* on 18 January 1915 for funds to be raised to help cover the cost of false teeth for men who could not pass the medical examination for enlistment until they had been fitted with dentures. Local dentists had offered their services free of charge as far as extracting or filling was concerned, but they could not meet the cost of the false teeth that were necessary in many cases. The Mayor invited subscriptions to a fund, which became known as 'Chompers for our Boys'.

Cardiff's Lord Mayor, meanwhile, was concerned that the various local organisations involved in fundraising should be coordinated to ensure efficient use of the monies raised. A meeting was arranged at the City Hall and invites were sent out to the leaders of all the known groups working on war relief matters. A request was made from the London promoters of the National Fund for Welsh Troops and the Mayor made a special appeal for funds to be raised for this organisation, commenting in the *Western Mail* that he was 'most anxious to adopt the best course that will bring about the best results in providing comforts for our countrymen serving in the armed service.'

As if to compound the wartime troubles endured by the local population, there was a measles scare in January 1915. In the town of Merthyr, where the outbreak was particularly bad, fifty people died in just one month and schools were closed for several weeks as a preventative measure. The illness raged for several months before it was brought under control.

Nevertheless, the people of Cardiff found brief respite from wartime life by visiting the New Theatre, where a tremendously successful production of *Babes in the Woods* was playing that season. Audiences flocked to see the pantomime and the press were ecstatic in their praise. 'There is not a wasted character in the entire cast,' praised the *Western Mail*. The review continued:

> Miss Madge Martin's London ballet of 24 young ladies in their various appearances during the evening give a brightness to the production which is quite bewildering in their gorgeousness. Nothing can be more pleasing to the parents and guardians of the children present than their smiling, chubby faces and screeches of laughter during the performance.

The pantomime ran for several weeks, and once the run was completed the entire cast made the rounds of the various hospitals in order to entertain the troops with song and dance routines from the show.

As 1915 rolled on and the reports from the various theatres of war filled the newspapers, the conflict began to gain a feeling of permanence. It was also forcing through far-reaching changes at home, altering some things formerly considered key elements of British life. For the first time women were drafted into occupations hitherto traditionally held by men, and council meetings up and down the country had to rush through emergency byelaws to allow women to enter certain professions. Although women were already a vital part of the workforce and no strangers to factory work, there had previously been limits on the kinds of work they were allowed to do. Now, with millions of men leaving their occupations and heading to the Front, the old ways of thinking were at odds with the demands of this new wartime world. Things began to change. In Cardiff, a crèche and day nursery was set up in the building next to the Woman's War Club in Cathays, to provide childcare for working mothers and enable more women to work.

Women tram conductors pose for photographs.

The second year of the War also saw the newspapers reporting on a social problem that many felt would put an additional strain on Britain's resources over the coming years. On 20 April 1915, the *South Wales Echo* carried a story under the headline 'War Babies, the Glamour of the Uniform':

> The problem of the 'war baby,' the illegitimate offspring of the soldier, baffles investigation at the very outset. Medical Men, clergymen, social workers, and Poor Law authorities everywhere confess their inability to make a statement, however conjectural, as to the size of the problem.

The article claimed that in one Yorkshire town where soldiers were stationed, it had been estimated that 150 'war babies' would be born within the next few months. Whatever the truth of such scare stories, people took them seriously and in Cardiff there was a movement urging the establishment of a new maternity hospital to take care of single mothers.

Earlier in the year, the newspapers had reported another novel event on the Home Front: German air raids. The first Zeppelin raid on British soil took place on 19 January 1915, when the airships L3 and L4 took off from Germany, each carrying thirty hours worth of fuel, eight bombs and twenty-five incendiary devices. The two airships had crossed the Norfolk coast and then the L3 headed south, while the other ship went north. Both dropped their incendiary devices to enable the pilots to better navigate towards their chosen targets, Great Yarmouth and King's Lynn, where they planned to drop their remaining bombs. Nine people were killed in the raid and the bombs damaged several buildings, but the attack also had far-reaching psychological consequences among the general population. People feared the possibility that more air raids would occur and that a German invasion by air was imminent. There were further air raids on British towns and cities as the War continued to rage – more than 100 in total, with a death toll of over 1,500.

Previously wars had been fought on foreign soil, but now conflict had come to the cities, towns and villages of mainland Britain. Wars

The thought of Zeppelins gave many people nightmares.

would no longer be fought just by men in uniform – every man, woman and child in the country had become a target. At the same time civilians were able to take a vital role in the War Effort, particularly the women drafted in to work in the munitions factories, along with the miners, dockworkers and shipbuilders in reserved occupations. As the War continued, the entire population would find itself harnessed to the War Effort in one way or another. In February 1918 food rationing – introduced after the German submarine blockade of the previous year had depleted food stocks – forced every single Briton to play their part by eking out their modest allowance.

There was excitement across Wales on 6 April 1915, when it was announced that two German prisoners of war had escaped from the camp at Llansannan. The North Wales Police led the search, assisted by the military, and the public were asked to be vigilant in towns and cities across Wales. The two missing men were identified as Lieutenant Von Sandersleben, aged twenty-four, and Hans Adler, aged twenty-eight. It was also noted that Adler spoke fluent English with a convincing accent, and a £10 reward was offered for any information leading to the recapture of the men.

Although it was expected that the escapees would head for the seaports of Liverpool, much of South Wales was put on alert. The two men were eventually recaptured a week later at Llanbedr, Barmouth. They were observed coming down the road by a river watcher named John Jones, who immediately ran to the local post office and telephoned the police. When confronted by the police the two men claimed to be French servicemen on leave, but this evasion was seen through and both men were quickly re-arrested.

Every day fresh reports of dramatic events were featured in the newspapers and the British public were becoming used to reading sensational stories. In May 1915, a German U-boat, the U-20, sank the Cunard ocean liner RMS *Lusitania*. The ship went down in just eighteen minutes, resulting in the loss of 1,198 people, with 761 survivors. The event horrified the world, turning public opinion against Germany, and it would eventually prove a key factor in America's declaration of war on Germany, as 128 of the dead were American

The New York Times reports on the sinking of the Lusitania.

citizens. The German authorities argued that the *Lusitania* had been a legitimate military target because it had been carrying weapons. The events surrounding the sinking of the *Lusitania* are still controversial today and continue to be fiercely debated by military historians.

For the British the sinking of a passenger cruiser was an outrage and the Press responded to the news with with revulsion. *The South Wales Echo* heavily condemned the Germans for their actions, calling the sinking, 'a war crime with no possible justification.'

Perhaps spurred on by the sinking of the *Lusitania*, recruitment drives continued across the country. *The South Wales Echo* reported that the Central Cardiff Recruiting Headquarters was now, out of necessity, employing many female clerks. Cardiff Post Office had also

Female clerks at Cardiff's Central Recruiting Office.

recently put out a press release stating that, for the first time, women would be employed as night workers. Provision had been made for any female staff working through the night to be returned home by taxicab afterwards, with their fares supplied by the postal service.

On 11 June 1915, the *South Wales Echo* stated that the biggest problem now facing the Allies was their ability to generate sufficient supplies of munitions. The main issue, the newspaper claimed, was to find the speediest methods of making and delivering munitions to the troops overseas. At this stage, Britain simply could not make munitions quickly enough to fulfil demand, and the military would have to step up production.

The authorities had initially suspected that the most significant challenge the country might face would be in getting enough men to enlist. This had not proven to be the case, as the men of the United Kingdom had responded in greater numbers than could have been hoped for. There was criticism of Lord Kitchener from some quarters for underestimating the needs of the War, but the newspaper felt that things would improve now that a Welshman, David Lloyd George, was to oversee the production of munitions.

Recruitment continued apace and it was reported in the *Glamorgan Gazette* that a Sergeant Franklin of the 17th Battalion would soon be rejoining his comrades after spending several weeks helping with the recruitment drive in Cardiff. Franklin was awarded a silver cane for his work at the recruiting headquarters. The presentation was made by the unfortunately named Lieutenant German, who made a statement to the *South Wales Echo* in which he praised the work of Sergeant Franklin for getting scores of Welshmen into uniform. Among those now putting on uniform was Pontypridd's star rugby player, Alister McGregor, son of the famous Duncan McGregor, who had taken a commission as a lieutenant in the Argyle and Sutherland Highlanders. Duncan McGregor was known for being a member of the 1905 original All Blacks rugby team.

June 1914 also saw the formation of a volunteer corps in Cardiff to protect civilians on the Home Front. Known as the Cardiff Civic Guard, the organisation was structured along military lines, and its establishment reflected the very real concerns provoked by the recent Zeppelin activity and fears of an eventual German invasion of mainland Britain. The organisation had its headquarters at Cardiff Arms Park and tents were erected, with an officer from the 3rd Welsh Regiment drafted in to ensure the organisation was turned into an effective military force.

The men were to be instructed in musketry, trench digging, and signalling, as well as military transport work. Numbers of recruits were initially expected to reach around 500, but the *South Wales Echo* noted that as so many men had come forward it seemed likely that a full battalion would be created. Once again Cardiff men had answered the call of their country without hesitation. Many of them were too old for active service, while others had minor disabilities which prevented them from joining the regular forces, and some were simply too young to enlist in the army. By joining this volunteer corps these men could serve their country to the best of their abilities.

Regardless of the high numbers of men enlisting for military service, more were still needed at the Front. Lance Corporal W. Brown, whose wife and children resided in Cardiff's Llanelly Street, while he served in the 88th Company with the British Expeditionary Force in France, wrote an open letter to the *South Wales Echo* addressed to the 'Boys of Cardiff':

> As I was reading the 'Echo' provided to me by my very good friend, Mr Chamberlain, I was more than surprised to hear of Sergeant Franklin's meeting at the Cardiff Exchange. It is terrible that a hero such as Corporal Thomas of the Welsh Regiment who is out here for the third time while there are slackers at home. The sooner the compulsion comes, the better, for it is certain that every man is needed. In my company we have 20 Cardiff boys and I am father to them all. Darkie Thompson from Bertram Street and C Canterbury the pigeon flyer from Grangetown are with us. I make this appeal on our King's birthday – God bless him. Are the boys of Cardiff ashamed to join up or – well, I don't like to use the word – Cowards.
>
> Don't for God's sake let Cardiff be known as The Slacker's City. We want every fit man to come and join and fight the scum, which the Allies are opposed against. If it were merely men we are fighting it wouldn't be so bad but we are up against the most cunning class of people the world has ever known. Well I am closing now because we have a few hours leisure and are going to have a game of cricket. Let all inquiring friends know that all is well with the boys from Cardiff. Thank you also for as good an evening paper as, 'The Echo,' and accept this letter as an echo from France.

The Corporal Thomas of the Welsh Regiment that he referred to, had recently returned to the Front after recovering from wounds sustained in battle. However, Brown's claim that Cardiff men were shirkers was unfounded. Although recruitment rates were no longer as high as they had been during the first few months following the outbreak of war, a steady stream of men were still being processed by the recruitment offices. In the week preceding the publication of the letter, many more Cardiff men had enlisted and they would continue to do so, although as the War dragged on and the casualty lists grew longer, the prospect of conscription became inevitable.

As the response to the army recruitment drive slowed throughout the summer months of 1915, the Government was reluctant to start forcing men into uniform. The fact that the British Armed Forces were made up of willing men was a matter of national pride, and this professional army of volunteers was one of the things that distinguished the country from its European neighbours. For the moment the

Promoting a recruitment rally.

British Government determined to push their recruitment message, in the hope that men would continue to come forward. The press helped to stoke up the patriotic fervour, with headlines repeating even tenuous rumours of German atrocities, such as 'Germans Slaughter Women and Children', or 'We must stop the Hun enslaving the world'.

In October 1915, a huge recruitment rally was held in Cardiff's Sophia Gardens, alongside a series of public meetings across the city. The rally included a pageant of thousands of soldiers and the 3rd Welsh Regiment band. Alongside these soldiers marched the special constabulary, members of the Red Cross and the staff of the city's recruitment centres. Wounded soldiers also attended the rally, and it was reported that some of these men gave rousing speeches beseeching the fit and able men of the city to take up their duty and join the great fight. The Dowlais Male Voice Choir sang at the rally, as well as the choir of the 7th Welsh Regiment. Recruiting cars travelling the city roads with a brass band marching in front of them. It was a patriotic spectacle for the people of Cardiff and encouraged a great many men to enlist.

Some Cardiff recruits were spurred on to join up by a more sombre event. On 5 October 1915, local people were shocked to learn that the city's popular MP, Lord Ninian Crichton-Stuart had been killed in action while leading the 6th Battalion of the Welsh Regiment during the Battle of Loos. Born in 1883, Lord Ninian was the son of the third Marquess of Bute. He had first entered politics in his native Scotland, before being elected MP for Cardiff in 1910. Known as a tactful and caring man, it was said that on the battlefield Lord Ninian's first concern had been for the safety of his men. Ninian was one of six members of parliament who were killed in the Great War.

Although many Cardiff men had already lost their lives, a genuine wave of sorrow was felt throughout the city at the loss of Lord Ninian. Cardiff City's former football ground, Ninian Park, was later named after him.

Lord Ninian had kept his seat as MP for the united boroughs of Cardiff, Cowbridge and Llantrisant when he volunteered for foreign service with the 6th Welsh Territorials. In addressing his men before leaving for the Front, Lord Ninian reportedly said, 'I am prepared, as I am sure you are to lay down my life for my country if required.' His soldiers had loved him, the *South Wales Echo* reported, regarding him more as a comrade than a commanding officer. The newspaper also noted that Ninian had, 'died a magnificent death, setting an example that made one proud to be British.'

When the Battle of Loos commenced on 25 September, it was the biggest British offensive yet launched on the Western Front. The battle was notable for the first use of poison gas by the British, and its objective was to aid the French in breaking through the German defences in Artois and Champagne. However, the German forces managed to hold their positions, despite significant losses on both sides. Lord Ninian was killed by a sniper during the battle, shot through the head while leading the 6th Welsh on a night attack on 2 October 1915.

The statue of Lord Ninian Crichton-Stuart in Gorsedd Gardens, Cardiff.

Private Norton of the 6th Welsh described his death to the *South Wales Echo*: 'Our late colonel, Lord Ninian, stood brave and bold until every man returned to safety. He was shot through the forehead and died a death worth dying. He was one of the best and we shall miss him.'

There was yet more unsettling news that October, when a man from Pontypridd was charged under the Defence of the Realm Act for making pro-German statements in a public house. William Thompson, a coal miner living in Rhondda Road, was said to have visited the Park Hotel and, while in a drunken state, to have told a soldier that he would be shot. 'I will live longer than any man here,' Thompson was reported to have said. 'I am pro-German. The biggest men are pro-German.' At that point that two men tried to attack Thompson, but he was a large man and fought them off. However, a Corporal Lloyd and a Private Lynch wrestled with Thompson, managed to overpower him and took him to the local police station.

When questioned by the police, Thompson told them that it was true, he was indeed pro-German. He also said that the men who had real power in Britain were also pro-German, and that the Germans were winning the War. Thompson later regretted his words and told the stipendiary at his trial that he had been drinking all day, going from public house to public house, and as a result was in an argumentative mood. He claimed that he had nothing against the King and was not in fact pro-German. He was sentenced to three months' hard labour, with the stipendiary remarking that Thompson had brought this all on himself by failing to control his drinking.

The was had by now gone on longer than anyone had initially expected, and was proving to be far more costly in terms of human life than even the most pessimistic could have predicted. The realities of life in a country at war were starting to hit home and, for the first time, the numbers of men volunteering for service were beginning to fall.

CHAPTER 4

The War Intensifies

Towards the end of 1915, with rising concern over the dwindling numbers of men voluntarily signing on for military service, the Government came up with a novel scheme that would enable them to identify those whom they considered were not fulfilling their responsibilities to King and Country. At the same time, this scheme would protect men who were willing to enlist but had failed to enter the forces on medical grounds.

The Secretary of State for War declared that khaki armlets would be issued to various groups of men across the country, including: those who had enlisted for service but had been put on reserve, until they were called up; men who had volunteered but failed to meet the medical requirements for service; men who had been invalided out of the services with good character; and those discharged due to injury or other medical issues. There was also another, slightly different class who would receive the armlets: men whose important business or family interests excused them from service. The third class consisted of those engaged in vital war work on the Home Front. Initially there was to be a distinctive mark on the armlets to identify each of the three classes. The armlets became known as 'Derby Bands' after Edward Stanley, the 17th Earl of Derby, who had recently been made the Government's Director General of Recruitment.

Further measures were still under discussion. "I know how many men I want and how many I want for munitions. I have their names and the numbers of their doors, and if they do not come I will fetch them," Lord Kitchener had told a Labour conference held in Manchester in October of 1915. It was a clear indication that compulsory service was being considered, but still the Government were reluctant to introduce conscription.

In the meantime, women continued to swell the ranks of the industrial workforce, replacing the men who joined up. By late 1915 twice as many women were working in munitions than men, freeing a lot of potential recruits who had been previously tied up with this vital work. Yet, understandably, a great deal of men were reluctant to enlist, recognising that the trenches on the Western Front were claiming a staggering amount of lives and the War looked set to continue for some time.

Recruitment posters stressed patriotic sentiments.

It was becoming increasingly evident that Britain could no longer rely on a steady supply of willing volunteers to take up arms. Although the standards for enlistment had been lowered, according to Government estimates there were around two million men of age to enlist who were not yet in uniform.

Calls for British men to enlist now took on a more menacing edge, and the Press began using negative quotes from unnamed Government sources, printing remarks accusing those 'who failed to answer the call to arms' of being 'cowards and shirkers'. Newspapers were filled with sensational stories designed to provoke men into joining the armed forces. 'The Huns are crucifying women and raping young girls to death,' was one such headline, printed in the *Daily Mail*, while another report in the same newspaper claimed that Germans troops had 'hacked up young babies and impaled them on their lances'. Most of these stories were complete fabrications and the authorities knew this, but they often promoted them in the hope that such rumours would sway public opinion and result in more recruits. The *Daily Mail* went one

Female wartime munitions workers.

step further and, in 1915, positioned the slogan, 'The paper that persistently forewarned the public about the war', beneath its masthead.

Not all reports of German atrocities were pure inventions, however. In October 1915, British nurse Edith Cavell was executed in German-occupied Belgium. 'Martyrdom of English Nurse,' asserted the *South Wales Echo* on 18 October 1915. Edith Cavell had aided Belgian soldiers seeking to escape to England by hiding them in her house, providing them with money and addresses in England and Wales, and even helping to smuggle them across the border. This was considered a very serious crime during wartime and the German military court found her guilty and sentenced her to death by firing squad. The *Echo* described her execution in a Brussels garden in lurid detail. Faced by the six-strong firing squad, the paper claimed that the blindfolded

Edith Cavell, photographed during happier times with the dogs she adored.

nurse, trembling in terror, had collapsed to the ground before a shot was fired. According to the *Echo*, a German officer then calmly walked over and shot her through the back of the head.

The newspaper went on to compare Edith Cavell with Florence Nightingale, and on the morning following the reports of her death every single eligible young man in Cavell's home village in Norfolk was said to have joined up for military service. 'This will settle the matter of recruitment once and for all,' the Bishop of London, Arthur Ingram was quoted as saying in the *Daily Mirror*. 'There will be no need for compulsion after this.'

In actuality, despite Edith Cavell's powerful story, the Government still found that men were still not coming forward to enlist in sufficient numbers. There was one last push to avoid conscription when Lord Derby requested that all men should come voluntarily attest to their willingness to fight. Under his new scheme, married men would only be called up if the supply of single men had been exhausted. Although hordes of married men, safe in the knowledge that they would not be sent to war, immediately signed up, only a little over 300,000 single men did so – far less than had been hoped for by the authorities. It now seemed that the only way to raise a sufficient army would be through conscription.

There was opposition to the very end, with the Labour Party and Trades Union Congress dead against the idea. Many politicians felt that forcing men into uniform was a clear admission of moral bankruptcy and it would also result in a weaker army. However, the appalling casualty rates meant that the measure could no longer be postponed. The argument continued to rage through the closing months of 1915, until the Military Service Act of January 1916 introduced compulsory military service for all men aged between 18 and 41. The only exemptions would be granted to men carrying out work of national importance, the disabled, and those able to show that their families would endure severe economic hardship should they join up.

The social reformer Beatrice Webb famously stated that, having closely followed the Munitions Act, the Defence of the Realm Act, and the curtailment of many peacetime labour rights, the new Act was the latest in a series of measures that placed Britain in 'a servile state'. She had a valid point: the country was now a very different place, and some things would never be the same again. By the time the War ended, the Government was not only able to determine which of its citizens should wear a uniform, but also the wages they could earn, whether or not they were entitled to a pension, and even, with the advent of rationing, what they ate.

While conscription was still several months off, the *South Wales Echo* had reported that 17,000 men in Cardiff had not signed up for service, despite being eligible to do so. The figure was based on a

Government estimate that across the country 1,900,000 eligible men were not yet in uniform.

A 59-year-old sergeant, Alfred Keeling from the Rhondda Valleys, who was serving in France wrote to the *Echo*, stating that he had answered Kitchener's call. After being examined by a doctor in Tonypandy, and found to be in good health, he had reported to Maidstone and joined the West Kent Regiment. 'I was with the regiment at Loos and Hulluch,' the veteran soldier boasted, and he had also recently served in the trenches. 'If I can fight at my age,' Keeling wrote, 'and I shall be 60 next March, then cannot some of the young ones still with you come out to help.'

There was excitement in the village of Pontygwaith when, on 21 October 1915, the thrice-wounded Corporal Tom Gronow, DCM arrived home to find a welcoming committee of thousands lining the streets. 'His escapes from death have been miraculous,' stated the *Pontypridd Observer*. 'His gallant deeds on the battlefield have won him promotion and the much sought after D.C.M.' The newspaper was correct in claiming that Gronow's survival was miraculous – he was first wounded at Ypres in 1914, when a bullet entered his chest and exited beneath his shoulder bone. Then, no sooner had he returned to active duty than he was shot in the knee at Festubert while running across No Man's Land to rescue wounded men, an act for which he received the DCM. Gronow gained his third wound at Hulluch, when he was hit by shrapnel, again while attempting to save others.

A modest man, Gronow was embarrassed by the reception. He told reporters that he had merely done his duty, nothing more and nothing less. When asked about the War, he commented:

> We have given the enemy a shock. There is a lot to be hopeful about. The German Army is not as powerful as it had been a year ago, the soldiers not as skilled as they once were, nor is the enemy artillery quite so intense.

Gronow, had served in the army for several years before the War and had been a reservist when hostilities had commenced. Prior to his latest

Female staff at Cardiff's Maindy Barracks, engaged in recruitment activities.

stint in uniform, he had been employed at the Davies and Sons colliery in Tylorstown and many of his former workmates were among those lining the streets to welcome their hero home.

As Lord Derby's scheme continued, the *South Wales Echo* reported that an additional 300,000 men would be needed each week across the country. The newspaper also revealed that a recent recruitment drive at Cardiff's Coal Exchange had resulted in a goodly number of men joining the services, though no exact figures were given.

The need for extra recruits became so great that a series of raids were carried out by the police and the military around Cardiff in late October 1915, designed to identify men of eligible age who had not signed up for military service. The raids were widely reported in the

The announcement of the Cardiff Pals Committee Gift Scheme.

Press, and the authorities apparently warned those they targeted that as conscription was coming it would be far better to join up willingly, before they were compelled to do so.

In December 1915 a committee of parents and friends of the Cardiff Pals met at Cardiff's Queen's Hotel to set up a gift scheme for the 11th Battalion. Around fifty people had been expected, but hundreds turned up, queuing patiently in order to give their own gifts for the Pals. A few days later, the organisation sent out packages including 10,000 Capstan cigarettes, 15lbs of tinned tobacco, tins of sardines and a hundredweight of boiled sweets.

Arthur Morris of Cowbridge Road, Cardiff, who had a son in the Pals, became the Honourable Secretary of the Pals Committee and later the editor of the *Pals Magazine*. This publication was produced monthly and contained information about fundraising, as well as articles relating to the Cardiff Pals and quotes from letters sent home from men serving at the Front. The magazine would later carry out details of actions taken by the Pals and report on their losses. The first issue came out in January 1916, with a cover price of 'What you like'. It was thereafter priced at 2d 'or more if you please', with all proceeds used to fund further issues, as well as to send out more goods to the Pals.

The magazine was invaluable, as it kept local people informed of events in Salonika, where the Pals were based from mid-1915 onwards. Letters sent to the magazine by those serving would often contain poetic lines about their desire to see Cardiff again or hear the chimes of the city's Cathedral. 'I suppose Canton is the same old spot!' one Pal wrote, while another dreamed of walking in the Cardiff countryside once more: 'What I wouldn't give to once again walk through the fields of Llandaff.'

The *Pals Magazine* would remain at the forefront of local fundraising activities throughout the War, and many issues were sent out to the Pals

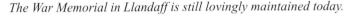

The War Memorial in Llandaff is still lovingly maintained today.

themselves in Salonika. The soldiers were delighted to receive the magazines and, judging by the letters they wrote to the editor, they were grateful for the support from home. As the War continued though, the magazine started to lose money and this, compounded by the worsening wartime paper shortage, meant that publication had to cease in 1917.

When Christmas 1915 arrived with no sign of the War ending, the British population maintained a cheery optimism despite the horrific stories filling the newspapers. However these reports cast a long, ominous shadow over the New Year ahead. Few now believed that hostilities would cease any time soon and, as 1916 dawned, prayers were said for those serving in what had turned into a war like no other.

CHAPTER 5

War in the Air

Eleven years before the outbreak of the Great War, the very first aeroplane trials had achieved a flight of just over 100 feet. By the end of the War, the first flimsy fighters had evolved into stunningly fast aerial fighters and heavy bombers. This was a new kind of warfare and it seemed fantastic and implausible to the general population, like something out of the popular novels of H.G. Wells.

In August 1914 squadrons of the Royal Flying Corps were sent over to France to support the British ground troops. Their duties were to observe enemy positions, as well as to identify and pinpoint large artillery weapons. The importance of the aeroplanes was realised on 22 August 1914, when a two-seater aeroplane, flown by Captain L. Charlton and Lieutenant V. Wadham, returned from a reconnaissance mission and revealed that Allied troops were in danger of being surrounded by the German II Corps. This information enabled the British troops to mount a preventative artillery attack. Air reconnaissance missions were extremely dangerous and RFC pilots had to contend with heavy machine-gun fire from German guns and quite often from their own side too, if their machines were mistaken for enemy aircraft. The pilots would often fly close enough to the German troops to retaliate by firing from the air with their revolvers.

As the trench warfare intensified, reconnaissance flights became of vital importance and photographic missions were carried out to gather pictures of enemy trenches, which could then be pieced together to create a map. Pilots would often drop grenades on the other side's trenches, and it was not long before machine-guns were fitted to aircraft for the observers or pilots to fire on the ground. In April 1915, an innovation called an interrupter gear was fitted to aircraft, allowing forward-facing machine guns to be used. This gear allowed machine gun fire to be perfectly timed, so that the bullets would travel through the propellers of the aircraft. This marked the arrival of aerial combat and a new phrase, 'Dog-fight', emerged.

A Dutchman, Anthony Fokker, perfected the interrupter gear and the Fokker Dr. I triplane he designed was flown by Manfred Albrecht Freherr Von Richthofen, otherwise known as, the 'Red Baron'. Von Richthofen flew this particular aircraft during nineteen of his eighty victories against Allied aircraft.

Manfred Albrecht Freiherr Von Richthofen, alias the Red Baron.

Pilots and observers became vitally important to both the Allies and the Central Powers. The Germans had entered the War with superior numbers of aircraft and by 1916 they had established more than twenty air training schools. It did not take the British and the French long to catch up, however.

Aircraft were increasingly used to bomb enemy ground positions, but this was initially very dangerous as pilots had to fly as low as they could before dropping their bombs. At this time there were no bombing sites and most missions were literally a hit or miss affair. Aerial bombing was far more successful in destroying communication lines and vital supply routes, such as telegraph lines, bridges and railways. Eventually, huge bombers able to carry 2,700 lbs of bombs for many miles were developed, which could be used against towns and cities situated far from the Front Line.

So important would aerial warfare become that in 1917 the British Army merged its air service with that of the Royal Navy, forming a single organisation: the Royal Air Force (RAF). By the end of 1918, the RAF had 4,000 combat aircraft and more than 100,000 personnel.

CHAPTER 6

1916 – Innovations in Destruction

Timeline of key events in 1916

January

8   The last British troops are evacuated from Gallipoli

27   Royal Assent is granted to the Military Service Act, the bill introducing conscription

31   Zeppelin fear sweeps the country after nine German airships bomb targets across mainland Britain

February

16   In response to the widespread public fear of Zeppelins, the War Office takes command of London's anti-aircraft defences

21   The Battle of Verdun, the longest battle of the War, commences

23   The British Government forms the Ministry of Blockade to investigate means by which financial pressure can be brought to bear on the Central Powers. Lord Robert Cecil is appointed Minister of Blockade

29   The Royal Navy sinks the German cruiser, *Greif,* losing one of its own warships during the attack

March

24   A British passenger ferry, the *Sussex,* is torpedoed whilst

travelling from Folkstone to Dieppe, with at least fifty of the 325 passengers killed

28 The Inter-Allied Conference is held in Paris and declarations of unity are made by Japan, Belgium, France, Great Britain, Portugal, Russia, Serbia and Italy regarding military, economic and diplomatic affairs

April

18 President Woodrow Wilson takes America a step closer to war by issuing an ultimatum to the German Government concerning their policy of unrestricted submarine warfare

24 The Easter Rising takes place in Dublin

25 A German battlecruiser bombards Great Yarmouth and Lowestoft

26 British Forces in Mesopotamia begin to advance on Baghdad

May

1 British Summer Time is introduced

4 The German Government renounces its policy of unrestricted submarine attacks due to pressure from America

15 The Air Board is formed to coordinate the Royal Flying Corps and the Royal Navy Air Service. Lord Curzon is named as Chairman

31 The Battle of Jutland begins

June

2 German forces attack Canadian sections of the Ypres Salient

5 HMS *Hampshire* is sunk by a mine off the Scottish coast, with Lord Kitchener among those lost

24 The Allies launch an artillery barrage along a 25-mile stretch of German trenches on the Somme

July

1 The Battle of the Somme, the most costly battle in British military history, begins

7   Lloyd George succeeds Lord Kitchener as Secretary of State
        for War

14   The Battle of Bazentin Ridge begins. The battle goes on to
        cost the Allies more than 9,000 men, while the Germans suffer
        losses of around 2,000

15   The Battle of Delville Wood, part of the Somme offensive,
        begins. Again large losses are sustained by the Allied forces,
        although official records on the individual battles are scarce,
        with casualties recorded as part of the overall offensive

19   The Battle of Fromelles is launched, in an attempt to lure
        German attention away from the Somme. The battle saw a
        record number of Australian deaths in a twenty-four hour
        period, with the loss of over 5,000 men of the Australian
        Brigades

20   British troops attack High Wood on the Somme, but fail to
        capture the area

August

28   Italy declares war on Germany

31   Germany suspends submarine assaults on non-military vessels

September

2   German airships attack London and other locations across the
        UK, in the largest air attack on the mainland during the War

10   The Allied offensive of Salonika begins

15   British tanks are used for the first time during the Battle of
        Flers-Courcelette

26   The Battle of Thiepval Ridge begins

October

1   The Battle of Le Transloy on the Somme begins

15   Germany resumes U-boat attacks

26   German torpedo boats attack the Dover Strait

November

13   The Battle of Ancre begins on the Somme

18   The Battle of the Somme ends
28   A single German aeroplane carries out the first daylight air raid on London, killing 162 civilians

December
7   David Lloyd George replaces Herbert Asquith as Prime Minister of Britain
12   Germany issues a peace note, suggesting terms with many compromises
18   America asks for statements of intent from warring nations
      The German attack on Verdun ends with the French holding their lines

Nineteen-sixteen was a watershed year, and the Battles of Verdun and the Somme marked the beginning of the end for the German Army. Yet, to those involved the massive battles fought that year were merely further horrors brought about by this war.

At the time, 1916 was viewed as a thoroughly miserable year by the British people. On 1 July, the first day of the Battle of the Somme, there was unprecedented loss of life; the figures appalled those on the Home Front and continue to resonate through the years. On that single day Britain and the Commonwealth suffered 60,000 casualties, one in three of whom were killed.

The year had begun with newspaper accounts of the conscription debate, as the new legislation progressed on its troubled route through Parliament. The *South Wales Echo* reported on New Year's Day on the resignation of Sir John Simon, the Home Secretary, who was vigorously opposed to conscription.

However, Simon's resignation had little effect. The Military Service Bill was duly passed, and now all single men of military age had to become soldiers by a given date under

Sir John Simon, resigned from his post of Home Secretary due to his opposition to conscription.

law. This loss of individual liberty was perceived as alien to the British way of life. Critics feared the act would destroy national unity, but with such appalling losses at the Front conscription was vital. The Act was eventually introduced with an overwhelming majority of MPs in favour and only 36 voted against it.

Overnight, all single men aged between 18 and 41 – apart from those doing work of national importance, the disabled and those who could prove they were the sole means of financial support for their dependants – were now required to comply when called up for active service. An amendment was swiftly made also allowing married men to be called up.

Just before the introduction of conscription, the South Wales Miners' Federation (SWMF) held several meetings during which it was decided that they would oppose the introduction of compulsory military service. Mr James Winstone, president of the Federation, announced that, in his opinion, the introduction of conscription was the single most foolhardy decision the Government could make. In a speech quoted by the *South Wales Echo* he passionately railed against the Act, saying, 'This was the biggest piece of foolishness under God's heaven. The promoters of this business would rather lose the war than lose conscription.' During an interview with the newspaper, Mr Winstone also commented that he simply wanted to maintain national unity, and there had never been a time in the history of the trade union movement when swift and decisive action had been more necessary. He ended with a warning to the authorities that he hoped common sense would prevail, because the feeling among the workforce was then so high that anything could happen.

As the protests over conscription accelerated, in January 1916 there were fears that the country's coalfields could grind to a halt, leaving the navy without enough fuel. Many newspapers were predicting that a general election would be forced before the month was over. On 5 January, the *Daily News* claimed, 'It is entirely possible, likely even, that we will see a General Election over the next few weeks.'

On 12 January, members of the South Wales Miners' Federation voted to down tools unless the conscription bill was withdrawn. An even more serious decision was made for delegates to approach the MFGB (Miners' Federation of Great Britain) at a meeting in London the following day, in which a ballot would be proposed for miners across the country to stop work in protest at the terms of the Military Service Act. 'The Welsh Executive are unanimous in their opposition to conscription in any form, for they believe that once it is passed it will be used against the working classes,' commented SWMF president James Winstone.

The threat of a national strike was extremely worrying for the Government and later on that year it would lead to David Lloyd George's coalition government taking state control of the British coalfields. However, at this point the Government was still led by Asquith, and it made a concession: necessary industrial workers, including miners, would be exempted from conscription. The Miners' Federation responded by stating that, although there was no weakening of their opposition to conscription, they did not feel it necessary to threaten the Cabinet with a strike at the present time.

Townsfolk in the Welsh Valleys town of Ton Pentre were distracted from worries about conscription when a grisly discovery was made on 1 February 1916. The bodies of two sisters, Hettie and Lillian Cogger of Tonypandy, aged eighteen and seventeen respectively, were found in a van they had recently been sleeping in after working late shifts. The sisters had been employed as superintendents at a shooting gallery in Ton Pentre, and it was said that they had decided to sleep in the van after work on the night of 31 January, because the shooting gallery was being kept open until 10.30pm in order to train new military recruits. When the girls were missed at work the following morning no alarm was initially raised, because their home in Tonypandy was a few miles distant and it was assumed that they were simply late. However, that afternoon the van doors were broken open and the two girls were found inside. The police were immediately called.

Hettie and Lillian had died from asphyxiation caused by the fumes of the oil lamps they had used to light the van. The inquest revealed that a bed had been placed at the back of the 10ft long, 5ft wide and 5ft high van, which did not have adequate ventilation. A verdict of death from asphyxiation was given. The girls may not have fallen in battle on foreign soil but they were still casualties of the War. The work they had been carrying out was of vital importance to the War Effort, and their deaths were caused by their dedication to it.

That same month Cardiff was placed on high alert for Zeppelin raids, after several recent attacks up and down the country. A special meeting of the town council was held to discuss the illumination of the city and the possibility of enforcing a blackout. A letter from the manager of the High Street Arcade Company, which owned both the Duke Street and High Street arcades, raised concerns that the brilliant

Lily Cogger of Tonypandy.

lighting throughout the city at night could act as a guiding beacon to enemy aircraft. The letter was handed over to the Chief Constable, as this was considered a police matter. The general opinion among the councillors was that it was highly unlikely that a Zeppelin would travel as far west as Cardiff, and that any panic was unfounded. Nevertheless, the council decided to look into the possibilities of anti-aircraft guns being placed in the city.

The population of Cardiff, like that of most major cities in the United Kingdom, was on edge, fearing imminent attacks from the air. The newspapers were filled with speculation on this new form of warfare and people were warned to be vigilant and look to the skies. Nerves throughout the city were by no means soothed when a story published in both the *Western Mail* and the *Echo* reported that a Captain Bennett-Goldney of the Royal Army Service Corps, had informed Parliament that the country was ill-equipped to deal with aerial raids. On 23 January there had been daylight raids on Dover, during which the airship managed to drop its load and escape without being challenged by a single British aircraft. The Zeppelin had taken everyone by surprise and the air force had not manage to scramble any aircraft in time. Assurances were given that an early warning system had been put into action, and that future raids would be met with fierce and deadly opposition.

On 8 March 1916 the first batch of conscripted men arrived in Cardiff for basic training at Maindy Barracks. They had come from Cardiff, Swansea, Merthyr, Porth and Pontypridd, and many more were expected to arrive on a regular basis. The *South Wales Echo* noted that conscripted men who had been called up would be subject to military law; any man refusing to follow orders would be treated as having committed mutiny and face court martial, with a possible death penalty.

The summer of 1916 was a particularly fine one, but those on the Home Front were constantly aware of the shadows of war. Day after day the newspapers were filled with reports of fierce fighting on all fronts. The Battle of Verdun had begun in February and would rage until December, with an average of 70,000 casualties each month.

On 1 July, the Battle of the Somme began. The British Army on the Somme comprised a mixture of the remnants of the pre-war Regular Army and 'Kitchener's Army', which consisted of many of the Pals Battalions. The incredible losses on the Somme would have a profound impact on Britain, and today the battle is seen as one of unparalleled slaughter for negligible gains. On 7 July, the 16th Welsh Battalion (known as the Cardiff City Battalion), along with other Welsh units, took part in an assault on Hammerhead at Mametz Wood. Their right flank was exposed to machine gun fire and heavy losses were sustained; more than 150 men died, with casualties numbering many times that. Among the dead were Welsh rugby internationals Dick Thomas and John Williams.

'On the Somme, the Cardiff City

The Big Push brought increasingly shocking images of the War to the Home Front.

The Mametz Wood Memorial depicts a Welsh dragon holding barbed wire.

Battalion died,' recalled one survivor, William Joshua, (quoted by Colin Hughes in his 1990 book, *Mametz*).

In September the film, *The Battle of the Somme*, which featured footage from the Somme, came to Cardiff and people queued around the block for each showing at the city's Park Place Cinema. The film had been shown to the King, and the makers claimed that it was free of all trickery and thus fully authentic, though it presented an incredibly patriotic viewpoint which skirted over the huge British losses and emphasised Allied victories. The film would also be shown at most of Cardiff's cinemas, as well as those throughout the surrounding areas, and it could be considered in modern terms to have been a blockbuster.

The interest in it was also spurred by the fact that it featured tanks – something few civilians had seen at this point.

Throughout September 1916 there was an additional series of recruitment raids across Cardiff designed to round up those perceived as dodging conscription. Many column inches in publications across the country were devoted to shaming these men. Since conscription had been introduced there had been a change in attitude amongst the general population, and many protested against the compulsory nature of the Military Service Act. However, the military, together with the police, were unrelenting and routinely rounded up any conscript who had failed to report.

On 14 September there was excitement in the area when a German prisoner of war escaped from a Breconshire camp. A description of the POW was released to all the local newspapers: he was twenty-three years of age, named Leuckel and had been dressed in his German Army uniform when he escaped. Just two hours after his escape Leuckel was captured 10 miles away from the camp, when a group of plate-layers saw him stealing a coat and marched him to the nearest police station.

Two days later there was more uplifting news, when over 1,000 wounded soldiers from Cardiff's hospitals were treated to a fête at Sophia Gardens. There was a band and several boxing exhibitions, with free entry to all servicemen. The money collected from civilians would be given to the Interned Merchant Seamen's organisation, which was presided over by Cardiff's Lady Mayoress. The *South Wales Echo* reported that the organisation contained 700 men from Cardiff.

From mid-September onwards, the tone of newspaper editorials grew increasingly positive and expressed the hope that soon the German Army would be defeated. It was now clear that the Allied Forces were making significant progress in France. 'Whole Somme Front Advances,' the *South Wales Echo* reported on 8 October. The accompanying article outlined the progress made by the Anglo-French troops, while the same edition also claimed that many German soldiers were demoralised to the point of desertion. 'Want to desert wholesale,' the newspaper speculated, but this would prove to be mere wishful thinking.

Further optimistic articles included claims that the British had command of the air space over France, and that aeroplanes had been taking part in combat, with dog-fights above the areas of Verdun and the Somme. It was reported that four enemy planes had been brought down, and that six more had been damaged and forced to land behind enemy lines.

There was a major disturbance in Cardiff on 11 November, when a meeting of the Pacifist Society being held in the Cory Hall was stormed by protesters. The police were called, but by the time officers had arrived at the hall several men had been assaulted and the pacifist leaders had been thrown down a staircase, then trampled underfoot. The story ran in the Cardiff newspapers for several days, and eventually the chain of events became clear.

The meeting had been well under way in the hall, when a group of around fifty anti-pacifists arrived outside carrying patriotic banners. Chants were shouted in which the pacifists were called 'cowards' and 'traitors'. An hour later, the anti-pacifists stormed the hall but the meeting continued despite their presence. At around 2.40pm several speakers took the stage and shortly afterwards pandemonium broke out. More and more protesters stormed into the hall and a huge fight ensued, with many of the pacifist on the stage being tossed down the stairs by the mob. It would take police some time to restore order and the general opinion was that the protesters had taught the pacifists a lesson. 'They had got what they deserved,' one newspaper jeered.

Afterwards, it was claimed that the anti-pacifists had been acting under the influence of alcohol. Cardiff MP J.H. Thomas, who had been at the meeting, told the *South Wales Echo*: 'You cannot fight against a force that is led by the influence of beer. I offered the leader of the protesters ten minutes on stage to put their point across, but this was refused.'

The pacifist movement was growing at this time, not only in Wales but across the entire nation. However, with so many people having recently lost loved ones in the War, and thousands of men facing compulsory call-up, a large proportion of the public considered the pacifists to be anti-British or even cowards. Several arrests were made after the incident in Cory Hall, but not one case came to court.

Towards the end of November 1916, the Press began claiming that Germany was now in such straits that its Government had imposed a levy on every man and woman in the country, and placed them under the command of the military. There were also stories suggesting that Germany was preparing to construct a massive air fleet, which would lead to an immense aerial battle. German women were allegedly being made to work on the construction of these air machines, while Belgian prisoners of war were put to work in German factories and mines. The British took heart from reports implying that Germany was close to breaking point, however insubstantial they were later revealed to be.

On 1 December 1916, all coalfields in the United Kingdom came under Government control. This was an unpopular move and so the Government immediately awarded the miners a 15 per cent increase in their wages, pending the results of an audit into the rising costs of coal production. While all this was going on, there was a crisis within the Government and on 2 December the Prime Minister, Herbert Asquith, had a protracted meeting with the King. David Lloyd George had also recently resigned from his role as Secretary of State for War, over claims that not enough was being done to ensure that Britain won the War.

There was much political wrangling going on behind the scenes. Lloyd George was a popular politician and this placed a lot of tension on Asquith as Prime Minister. No one expected him to step down to make way for Lloyd George, but that is what happened. 'Lloyd George Prime Minister,' the *South Wales Echo* headline proclaimed on 8 December. The general response to the change of prime minister was positive. The people of Wales in particular welcomed the news, for Lloyd George was a Welshman and said to be a far stronger personality than the ex-Prime Minister. It was hoped that the country could now get on with the business of winning the War.

David Lloyd George, the Welshman who was to lead the country in these dark times.

CHAPTER 7

The Cardiff Pals in Macedonia

Private Herbert Paine Smith started work at Cardiff docks as a nineteen-year-old clerk in 1910. Five years later, he found himself in Macedonia, proudly wearing the uniform of the 11th Battalion, Welsh Regiment, better known as the Cardiff Pals.

In November 1915, Herbert Paine Smith was stationed in the city of Salonika, which must have seemed terribly exotic to the young Welshman, with its white towers and minarets glowing in the sun. Paine Smith recalled many years later that the sunset would often send a red glow the shade of blood across the waterfront buildings. It was a place of great beauty and ethereal charm, with that unsettling but wondrous red glow occurring in both the evening and dawn skies.

The 11th Battalion had come a long way from the rat infested trenches of the Western Front, but if any of the men had thought their service here would prove easier than the conditions they had experienced in France then they were mistaken.

Salonika was most interesting; it was so obviously Eastern and mysterious; queer dark alleys; churches dating from the time when Christianity was young; wonderful pagan mountains; mosques and minarets; an amalgam of all races and all tongues. There one could see the Turk in his fez and baggy trousers, the

Herbert Smith (rear left), while serving with the Cardiff Pals in Salonika.

swarthy-kilted Greek, the Jew in dignified Gabardine as if he were Shylock himself come to life; handsome gypsy-like Serbs and Bulgars. Then the Allied Army itself – French, British, Italian, Russian, Serb, Indian, Chinese, never was so strangely a differing host of crusaders gathered together.

(Captain E. I. G. Richards,
11th Battalion Welsh Regiment, personal diary)

Greece had thus far remained neutral in the War, but the citizens of Salonika were unhappy about the Allied troops filling the streets and unafraid to display their displeasure. British soldiers were treated rudely at times and often ignored by local people. 'We were not welcome there, we were not welcome there at all,' Herbert Smith recalled in 1981. 'All we had were glares and stares from the Greeks.'

Another aspect of their posting was also troubling the Cardiff Pals. When the troops started receiving mail from home they heard of a rumour then circulating in Cardiff, that the Pals had been sent to Salonika because the battalion had staged a mutiny in France, refusing to go over the top at the Battle of Loos on the Western Front. This was entirely untrue, as the Battalion had not been stationed at Loos, but recalled from France and sent to Salonika to form a vital part of the Macedonian Campaign. The rumours unsettled the men to such an extent, however, that Colonel Crowley was forced to write to the Cardiff newspapers to issue a categorical denial of the mutiny story, which was published in both the *South Wales Echo* and the *Western Mail*.

The Cardiff Pals' daily routine consisted of intense training sessions, followed by discussions on tactics, which often went on until late in the evening and left the men both mentally and physically exhausted. Colonel Crowley exerted a brutal influence over his men and oversaw their rigorous training. Although he was not well-liked among the men he commanded, they understood that achieving physical fitness was of vital importance before they moved into the mountainous Front Line.

The Pals did not stay long in Salonika and they were soon heading out into the Macedonian mountains, which were far higher than even the hilliest parts of Wales. Here, the type of landmarks these men would have been familiar with in their own land – trees, roads towns and villages – were entirely absent. Instead they stumbled upon poverty-stricken settlements in a landscape that was scorching in summer and freezing in winter and constantly full of annoying, often dangerous insects.

This first winter the Pals spent in Macedonia was a particularly bad one. On the night of 26 November, a group of twelve men had to be carried back from forward the trenches. Despite their greatcoats, the cold had severely affected the men and several were close to losing consciousness. Oxo cubes and coco powder were hastily brewed and administered, yet Colonel Cowley showed no sympathy for their plight and continued to impose a harsh regime. There was no distinction in his mind between the criminals he had dealt with in civilian life as a prison warden, and the volunteers fighting for their country that he now commanded.

On one occasion during morning exercises Cowley mustered his men by driving them into the snow like husky dogs, swinging a riding crop over their heads and howling like a wolf. He had a fanatical belief in fitness and he pushed the men to the limits of their endurance. He would take the battalion on 20-mile marches, while he followed behind on horseback, as was his privilege. If any man dropped out during the marches he would be put on a charge. Cowley would charge men with disobeying orders if they so much as swayed with fatigue when he told them to keep still after a march.

Cowley's most controversial move was to introduce Field Punishment Number One, a brutal punishment which consisted of strapping the offender by the wrists and ankles to a gun wheel, with his heels dangling just off the ground. This came to be known as 'crucifixion' and it has been alleged that the punishment was often carried out within range of enemy fire. Cowley reportedly had one private put on the wheel for answering an officer back, and another simply for losing a button on his shirt.

One afternoon during a snowstorm, four men were strapped to trucks which were then drawn into a circle. This action provoked a severe argument between Cowley and Captain Tom McCosh, the Battalion Medical Officer. McCosh told Cowley that the men should be cut down because he considered them to be in real danger of frostbite, but Cowley refused his request. 'I must have discipline,' he asserted. Furious about this ill-treatment of the men, McCosh then acted on his own initiative, signalling the 77th Brigade HQ, to inform them of what was happening. Shortly afterwards a staff officer arrived and had a blazing row with Cowley, resulting in the release of the offenders.

Herbert Paine Smith and Bjarne Nilson, known to their comrades as the 'Heavenly Twins'.

In 1916 Herbert Paine Smith became one of the last men in the British Army to suffer Field Punishment Number One. Charged with having thrown away a lice-infested shirt, he was promptly strapped to the wheel. Smith's best friend Bjarne Nilson was furious about the unjust punishment and, determined to join his friend in custody, he urinated in the company's lines to provoke Paine Smith.

> When we went out to Macedonia we were issued with just one shirt, and only those who went through it can understand what it is like to be lousy. We had so many lice on us that we just couldn't cope with them. We used to douse ourselves with a burning ointment that felt like a burning poker going across your body but it kept the lice down. At the same time it made your shirt oily and greasy. Well I threw my shirt away and I owned up to it. Our commanding officer (Cowley) treated us like common prisoners and I ended up with seven days' field

punishment. This meant that I was strapped to a gun wheel for a couple of hours a day. You did a couple of hours on the wheel and then for the rest of the day you were under close arrest.

(Herbert Paine Smith, unpublished reminiscences.)

In his next letter home, Smith told his mother of the punishment he had undergone. Mrs Smith was absolutely livid and wrote to her member of parliament about what had happened to her son. He, in turn, brought the issue before the House of Commons.

Long before this, on 20 December 1915, Cowley himself had written to Arthur Morris, the Editor of Cardiff's *Pals Magazine*. Cowley took a genial tone that was not borne out in his leadership style: 'I aim to make them my boys as well as your boys. Truly I cannot hope to do so with the charming personality of my predecessor Colonel Parkinson, but I have no doubt of achieving the same end.'

In March 1916, two sergeants, T. A. Marsh and F. I. S. Chant, took a great risk in writing to the editor of *John Bull* magazine to complain about Cowley's methods. The authors of the letter requested that the magazine should not publish their names and then went on to outline the problems they faced, with examples of the barbaric methods practised by Colonel Cowley. The letter informed the public that since Cowley had replaced Colonel Parkinson, the men of the Battalion were often being treated like criminals. Field Punishment Number One was being used on a regular basis they claimed, and the commanding officer had punished more than thirty men in this way since they had arrived in Salonika. The duration of the punishments varied between seven and twenty-one days. Several men had been punished with seven days of field punishment, simply because they had thrown away verminous shirts, yet if they had kept the shirts, then they would have infested everyone with whom they came into contact. The letter was never published for fear of provoking public anger and damaging morale on the Home Front. Instead it was handed over to the authorities.

On 18 April 1916, Colonel Cowley was recalled to Britain, officially for health reasons, and command of the Pals was handed over to Lieutenant Colonel H. J. Wingate. The men were jubilant at the news and in letters home many of them called their new commander a fine gentleman.

Now under a kinder commanding officer, the daily routine in Macedonia quickly became monotonous for the Pals. Few understood what they were meant to be doing there. Were they there to attack or defend? Not even their leaders seemed to know what their purpose was intended to be or why they were fighting Bulgaria. Among the British military authorities some believed that British troops should not have been committed to the Salonika theatre. The issue caused fierce arguments between the British and French. In December of 1915 the British Prime Minister considered recalling British forces to deploy them in France, but the French argued that the abandonment of Salonika would drive Greece into the arms of Germany,

Lieutenant Colonel H. J. Wingate took over command of the Cardiff Pals from the unpopular Colonel Cowley.

which could lead to the establishment of a German submarine base in the Aegean Sea. And so the Pals remained in this theatre of extremes, where the temperatures veered in winter to depths of 20 degrees and in summer blazed to over 100.

In August 1916, the Pals moved up to Jenikol in the mountains for trench duty and patrol work against the Bulgars. The Bulgars had been reinforced with additional German troops and stiff fighting was anticipated. The Pals dug a tunnel through the mountain, linking the frontal defensive trenches with the rear positions, which earned them much kudos from military leaders. In charge of digging the tunnel was Major C. Godfrey Jones, the ex- manager of Bwylfa Colliery in Aberdare, assisted in coordinating the digging by two privates from

Tonyrefail, D. C. Evans and Evan Morgan, who had both been miners at the Navigation Pit in Coedely.

That summer malaria took a heavy toll on the Pals, reducing their strength to 600 men by the end of August. Other units were hit even harder, with the 10th Irish reportedly losing nearly 100 men a day to the disease, many of whom would not recover sufficiently during the War to return to the Front Line. The disease would prove as deadly an enemy as the Germans and, as a result of losses, several units had to be merged.

'At one time or another all of the men had malaria but I never did. I don't know why but I never contracted the disease. I was the odd man out,' Herbert Paine Smith remembered many years later.

> I pitied those poor devils. I remember swilling men down who had temperatures of a 103, 104 even – really close to death. We'd swill them all over to bring their temperatures down and then the following morning they'd have to get up and go about their duties. I don't know how they managed it.

The end of the summer saw the Pals taking over the French line to the south of Lake Dorian, near Machukovo. Upon the hills overlooking the lake, which reached 1,500 feet at the highest points, the enemy troops had constructed a series of defensive posts. Between the Pals and the enemy was No Man's Land. This imposing enemy stronghold was attacked on 13 September 1916, with the 22nd Division targeting two hills overlooking Machukovo. They were supported by the 9th East Lancashires, who were to come in from the right flank, while the 11th Regiment sought to protect the left flank. The Pals were held in reserve and detached several men for stretcher bearing duty.

After the men moved out a heavy British bombardment targeted the hills. When the shelling lifted at 2.00am, the attack had been driven home and the objectives secured, but twelve hours later a vicious enemy counter attack began, which drove the British back to their original position. In all 586 British soldiers were either killed or wounded – a heavy loss considering the fact that their ranks had already been significantly trimmed by malaria. Enemy losses were also high and seventy soldiers from the German 59th Regiment were captured as prisoners of war. Nine men from the Pals were killed during the enemy counter-attack, while trying to bring in the wounded. These were: Privates P. V. Lewis, Thomas E. Theaker, P. V. Cooper, J.A. Gratton, J. Jones and G. Thomas, Corporal P. Reid and Lance Corporals A. J. Burland and W. R Morris.

The ultimate failure of the attack convinced the Allied generals that it was futile to attack enemy strongholds in such a way. In future attacks would have to be far subtler. Night raids were initiated, with men going in and causing as much damage as possible before quickly pulling back to their own lines. This called for clever planning and audacious acts of bravery, as the men were told to crawl to within earshot of the enemy, then to sprint the final few yards, and jump into the trenches with fixed bayonets and bombs, to kill or capture as many soldiers as possible before swiftly departing. This involved brutal hand-to-hand fighting, with enemy soldiers no longer viewed at a distance through the sight of a rifle, but face to face.

The Pals were among the units selected for the first of these night raids, and a group of men led by Sergeant Oscar Hubbard were sent out along with other raiding parties on 22 October. The aim of the mission was to raid the enemy trenches and each of the men taking part were issued with twenty grenades and a hatchet intended as a wire-cutting tool. The raid was a success but a horrific experience for the individuals involved. Sergeant Hubbard and his team threw grenade after grenade into dug outs filled with screaming men, while Private William Edward Smart bayoneted two Germans and took six prisoner.

The commanding officer, Lieutenant Colonel Wingate, wrote in his despatches: 'No troops could have behaved with greater gallantry or dash, and the operation throughout will add another page to the glorious history of the Welsh Regiment.' Many of the men involved in the raids received awards for their bravery. Private H. W. Lewis was given the Victoria Cross, after carrying an injured man through a barrage of enemy fire; Major Scott-Hopkins, who had led the series of raids, won the DSO; and medals were also issued to several other men.

Christmas 1916 saw the Pals enjoying a festive dinner of bully beef and biscuits, but one Pal regretted the lack of a more traditional meal. Herbert Paine Smith had been out on manoeuvres with his friend Bjarne Nilson, when they spotted a flock of geese on a frozen lake. The two men knew that they had only one chance of bagging a bird, as the flock would fly off as soon as the first shot was fired. They had to make the shot count, as Herbert remembered:

> I thought we could do something for the men, give them a decent Christmas dinner. We knew we only had one shot and I was the better marksman so I took it. I missed. I'd been through a sniping school, I was supposed to be a sharpshooter and I missed the bloody geese.

Private H. W. Lewis, VC.

The Pals were not going to let the event pass without some sort of celebration, however, and together with men from other units they passed the evening in singing carols.

The New Year saw the continuation of the night raids, but as time went on the enemy troops became much more cautious and the raids became more intermittent. In March there was a horrific gas attack, which took the Pals by surprise. Gas was feared by all soldiers at the time, most of whom would much rather face a bullet. A man could take days to die from gas poisoning, all the while screaming in agony before his lungs finally gave in. The Pals had experienced gas in France but this was much worse, as the Germans had recently developed an even deadlier form of gas. Men scrambled for their masks, choking as they bumped into one another in the frantic search, and several were killed.

The war in Macedonia was turning into a mirror of events on the Western Front, and throughout the early months of 1917 a stalemate ensued. The Allied forces could not progress and the Bulgarian forces, strengthened by German reinforcements, still held the mountain strongholds. To break the deadlock, that spring an offensive was planned to coincide with Allied pressure on the Western Front.

The Pals were held in reserve for this string of operations, but other units were not so fortunate. On 24 April 1917 the 7th Wiltshires attacked the Petite Couronne, but they were almost immediately pinned down by heavy shellfire, while the 10th Devonshire Regiment was virtually wiped out in the bombardment. At the same time, the 12th Wiltshire Regiment became trapped in a ravine and suffered heavy losses. Only minimal gains were made, yet at an alarming cost: more than 3,000 British soldiers were killed or wounded.

On 8 May there was another attack on the mountains, this time carried out by units from the 26th Division, with the Pals once again held in reserve, and there were more heavy losses on both sides as a result. The 12th Argyll and Sutherland Highlanders lost all of their officers; the 7th Oxford and Bucks were struck by heavy mortar fire. Other units directed to support them were ultimately driven back and, in total, over 1,000 British troops were wounded or killed during the offensive.

Although the Pals had avoided the bloodbath they continued to lose men to disease. It became standard practise to burn down the areas of long grass which served as breeding grounds for the malaria-carrying mosquitoes and on 3 August enemy shells killed three Pals while they were burning a large stretch of grass.

On 29 May, the Pals embarked on a daring night raid on an area nicknamed Machine Gun Hill. Lieutenant H. Lawson-Jones led the raid taking thirty men up into the hills with him. The men skirted a Bulgarian trench and attacked it from a slope at the rear. Sergeant Richards rugby-tackled a Bulgarian who came running towards them, and in the struggle he took a bullet through the head. The sergeant was the only man to lose his life in this particular attack and two scouts from the Pals, Herbert Paine Smith and his friend Bjarne Nilson, carried his body back to the British lines.

There were, however, moments of calm for the men stationed in Macedonia, and they passed their time between operations reading or playing cards.

The people of Cardiff rallied behind us and we would regularly
receive parcels from home. Smokes mostly but often books and
other treats. We were very grateful to the people back home. I
always had a book to read thanks to these kind people.
(Herbert Paine Smith, unpublished reminiscence.)

In September 1918, the reason for their presence in Macedonia
suddenly became clear to the Pals when they were instructed to take
part in a massive frontal assault on enemy lines. Ever since they had
arrived in Salonika the British Army had been covered by the concrete
observation post at the top of the Grande Couronne. The observation
post was thought to be unreachable, as the 100 yard stretch below it
was topped by barbed wire, and on each side of the post and at several
points on the lower hills there were well-concealed machine-gun posts,
known as the Hill, the Trassel, the Knot, the Tongue and the Blade.
High above all this, on the 2,000ft high Pip Ridge were enemy trenches
and tunnels skirting the area. This area was known as the Dorian Front
and now in September 1918, it remained in enemy hands and was
considered to be virtually impossible to take, after the failure of the
British spring 1917 offensive. The peaks were held by Bulgaria's best
fighting units, who looked down on Allied forces reduced to half
strength after three years of campaigning.

It was decided that the 11th Welsh would be responsible for taking
first the Tassel and the Knot, before moving on to join the main
assault on Grande Couronne itself. Unknown to the Pals, there had
been fierce arguments by the generals planning the attack, as some
felt that throwing fit men at the Bulgarian guns was close to legalised
murder.

Orders, however, were orders, and on the evening of 17 September
1918, members of the Cardiff Pals Battalion began to gather at their
company markers, situated approximately a mile away from the attack
start line. The men were told to get some sleep at first, as sentries would
awaken them at 2.00am. It is doubtful whether any of the men managed
to sleep, knowing the dangerous task ahead of them. Also, while this
was going on a 48-hour Allied barrage targeting the hills was reaching

a crescendo. The previous night several scouts, led by Herbert Paine Smith, had been sent out into the hills to place white tape on the gaps between the British wires, in order to guide the men when the attack took place.

A stray shell had hit Paine Smith, blowing off one of his fingers and tearing one of his legs apart. He was taken back to the British lines, regretting that he would not now be taking part in the long planned attack with the rest of the Pals. He later recalled the mixed emotions he experienced: 'I came back with a finger hanging off and my leg all bandaged up. A piece of my bone had been blown out of my leg. These injuries likely saved my life. It was now all over for me. I had done my bit.'

Assisting the Cardiff Pals in the offensive on Grande Couronne were the 67th Brigade of the 22nd Division, which comprised the 7th and 8th Battalions of the South Wales Borderers, and the 11th Battalion of the Welsh Fusiliers. At 2.00am the men were roused and they immediately set about getting their equipment together. Each of them would be equipped with a pack of items with a combined weight of more than a hundredweight (112 lbs or 51 kg), including a gas mask, pack, water bottle, bayonet, steel helmet and 120 rounds of .303 ammunition. The men were given their rum rations and at 2.45am the Pals moved forward to the start line.

The Allied barrage continued to pound at the enemy lines, and as the Pals waited for the order to attack they remained silent, many of them lost in private thought. It was not until 5.08am that the Allied barrage finally lifted and the order to advance was given. Captain Enyon, the commander of B Company, kicked his rugby ball at the enemy – a symbolic gesture made by a fanatical rugby player – and the Pals started to move up the hill.

It was not an easy climb and the difficulties were exacerbated by the fact that the men were all wearing gas masks and carrying heavy equipment on their backs. To add to these obstacles, the ground beneath their feet was often slippery and they also had to contend with fierce enemy fire as they tried to cross the wire towards the Tassel and the Knot. Captain Enyon became tangled in the wire and he lay across the razor-sharp wire, in severe pain from shrapnel wounds. Close by him was Jim Charles, who had been hit in both the arm and leg. Another Pal, Jack Hillier, attempted to pull Enyon off the wire but he was struck by the explosion from a Bulgarian grenade and collapsed himself. The three men remained there, injured and alone – a fact which may have ensured their subsequent survival.

Up at the Tassel and the Knot, Cardiff Pals were dying by the score, mown down by the fierce machine gun fire or blown to pieces by the grenades hurled by the counter-attacking Bulgarians. Private Izzie Shibko, still carrying the axe he had used in the earlier attack on Machine Gun Hill, was shot through the head as he crouched down during a break in the advance. By 8.00am the 11th Welsh had ceased to exist, as the men lay dying and wounded on the slopes of the Tassel and the Knot.

Every battalion that attempted to rush the Couronne that morning was slaughtered. Greek forces coming in from the left of the Pals were also decimated. Captain Norman Hughes, the son of the Bishop of Llandaff, rallied together one of the sections at the bottom of a gully and led them through the cloying smoke towards the enemy trenches. They too were mown down, with Captain Hughes's body later discovered stripped naked, his boots and clothing taken by the Bulgarians. (The grisly practice of collecting war souvenirs from the fallen was common to all sides.) The massacre continued, and when it was all over not a single Cardiff Pal had come back, nor had any of the men from the 7th South Welsh Borderers or the 11th Royal Welsh Fusiliers.

The pride of Cardiff had gone to war one sunny September morning in 1914 and now, four years later they lay dead or dying, as the dawn began to rise over Grand Couronne. The few Cardiff Pals who survived the War formed the Pals Old Boys Association. The association was very active in the years following the War, with the highlight of their year being the annual

Captain Norman Hughes, son of the Bishop of Llandaff.

dinner at Cardiff's Park Hotel. As time went by, fewer veterans were able to attend and the last event was held in 1969.

*   *   *

In 1981, many years after the battle that claimed so many of his comrades, Herbert Paine Smith sat down with his son, Major Bob Smith, to record his memories of the time he spent with the Cardiff Pals. These recordings formed the backbone of this chapter.

'Those men I knew, those I served with were among the best kind of men,'
                      Herbert Paine Smith.

Herbert Paine Smith, photographed in 1981.

CHAPTER 8

Women at War

Changes made to British employment law during the First World War would forever transform the country's workforce. Census records show that on the outbreak of war only one in every four women worked, with a large proportion employed in domestic service or nursing roles. However, as jobs traditionally held by men, such as skilled jobs in factories, became vacant increasing numbers of women fulfilled the demand for labour.

By the end of the War, more than a third of Britain's women were in paid employment as tram drivers, gas workers, farm hands, office clerks, police officers and munitions workers. Of course women had always worked in many different industries, but the War dramatically altered the female role in the workplace. For the first time women workers were seen as indispensable.

The coal mines of the Welsh Valleys did not constitute the only important local industry during the First World War; Cardiff was surrounded by rich agricultural land and the Women's Land Army, formed in 1917, became a vitally important part of the labouring workforce. By 1918 there were 20,000 volunteer Land Girls serving across the United Kingdom.

Following the introduction of conscription, Green Farm in the Ely area of Cardiff was run mainly by female farm hands. The farm boasted a large dairy herd which supplied milk to the local hospitals. One Land Girl from the Ely District, Agnes Greatorex, left a life in domestic

Women's Land Army recruitment poster.

service to work on the land. When interviewed by the BBC in 1994 for the *Our Lives* television series, she recalled: 'Every morning we would get up at five o'clock and milk a hundred cows. We would then take the milk to Glan Ely Hospital.'

Although there was an obvious demand for women to take over the jobs now left vacant by male workers had been called up, it was still a contentious issue. Careful negotiations were held with the trade unions before women war workers were hired on a large scale, and these talks resulted in women being paid much less than their male counterparts for doing the same jobs.

Nevertheless, the fact that women were now joining the workforce in greater numbers than ever before was a social revolution. Prior to the War, the women's suffrage movement had campaigned for the right of women to vote, and although their activism had been suspended for the duration of the War, they and millions of female war workers played a key part in the conflict. During the War, the leaders of the suffragette movement concentrated on helping the Government to recruit women for jobs previously reserved for men. In July of 1915, with the support of Lloyd George's Ministry of Munitions, Emmeline Pankhurst led a march of tens of thousands of women through the heart of London, demanding that women should be allowed to do war work. A newsreel report carried the boast: 'The British Lion is awake, so is the Lioness.'

Women soon embarked on munitions work in wartime factories across the country, and more than 200,000 were engaged in the filling and manufacture of shells alone. At many of these munitions factories, known as National Filling Stations, a large proportion of the workforce were female, and elsewhere local women were also employed in making rifles and producing the chemicals used in poisonous gas.

Eventually, women were even recruited to work in certain sections of the army, freeing men to serve at the Front. In 1917, the Government

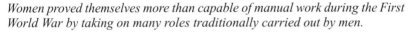

Women proved themselves more than capable of manual work during the First World War by taking on many roles traditionally carried out by men.

announced the establishment of a new voluntary service, the Women's Auxiliary Army Corps (WAAC), in which women would be able to carry out military service as telephonists, waitresses, cooks and even as instructors in the use of gas masks. The more traditional section of the military, however, felt that it would be counter-productive to give women commissions, and so the women in charge were given the non-commissioned ranks of 'controller' and 'administrator'. Over 57,000 women nationwide served in the WAAC during the conflict.

When the War finally ended, the proportion of women in employment initially fell, as men returned to their old jobs and women war workers were dismissed to make way for them. However, the seeds of social change had been sown and throughout the ensuing decades something positive would gradually emerge from the dreadful days of the Great War.

WAAC recruitment poster.

CHAPTER 9

1917 – A Long and Costly Struggle

Timeline of key events in 1917

January

10   The Allies state peace objectives in response to a request from the American President, Woodrow Wilson

February

1   Germany resumes unrestricted submarine warfare

3   America severs diplomatic ties with Germany

11   British forces capture the city of Baghdad

14   The Allies cautiously advance as the Germans continue their withdrawal to the Hindenburg Line

17   Allied troops occupy the town of Bapaume following the German retreat

26   The first Battle of Gaza is fought between British and Turkish forces

      The President of the United States, Woodrow Wilson, requests permission from Congress to arm American merchant vessels to enable them to defend against potential German attacks

April

6   America declares war on Germany

9   The Battle of Arras begins
12   The American military announces the arming of merchantmen
       by executive order, after failing to win approval from Congress
17   The second Battle of Gaza begins

May

10   Britain introduces the convoy system in a bid to defeat
       German U-boats
15   The Arras offensive ends. As a result the Allies gain a great
       deal of ground with limited casualties
23   German Gotha bombers unsuccessfully attack London

June

7   The Battle of Messines Ridge, south of Ypres begins. The
       Allies inflict large losses on the Germans
15   America introduces the Espionage Act in order to combat
       German spies
24   The first contingent of American soldiers arrive in France
27   Greece enters the War on the side of the Allies

July

6   T. E. Lawrence and Arab forces capture Aqaba
16   Third Battle of Ypres begins
31   The Battle of Passchendaele begins

August

2   The Ypres offensive is temporarily suspended due to bad weather
17   General Smuts publishes a report on British air defences. This
       report sows the seeds for the establishment of the Royal Air
       Force, as he recommends that a single air force should be
       formed

September

20   The Battle of Menin Road begins

October
26   Brazil declares war on Germany

November
10   Passchendaele is taken by the Allies
20   The Battle of Cambrai begins, during which a large number
        of tanks are used
25   Germany withdraws from Portuguese East Africa
30   German troops launch a counter offensive at Cambrai and
        eventually regain much of the ground lost to the Allies

December
3   Haig orders a retreat from Cambrai
8   The Battle of Cambrai ends with a limited Allied victory
9   Jerusalem is captured by the Egyptian Expeditionary Force,
        losing the Central Powers a great deal of territory
22   Russia opens peace negations with Germany

Nineteen-seventeen began with hopes of peace but, as the *South Wales Echo* reported on 1 January, the British Government rejected German peace proposals, in agreement with the Allies. In the same edition, the *Echo* revealed that a recent meeting of the South Wales Housing and Development Association had come to the conclusion that at least £500,000 should be provided by the Government when the War ended for the building of new homes and the construction of roads around Cardiff. The paper also recounted the ending of a local crime wave, after an Aberdare schoolboy had been sentenced to three strokes of the birch by the courts for stealing a purse containing 25 shillings. The boy was believed to be responsible for a string of pickpocketing offences which had plagued the area over the previous weeks. The birch was seen, even by this period, as an outdated and uncivilised form of punishment but, with the War raging, the courts had no time for lawlessness of any sort.

In 1917 the hot topic for British civilians was food rationing, which became increasingly likely as shortages worsened and German submarines targeted British merchant vessels once more. Prior to the

War, Britain had imported almost 60 per cent of its food and the German high command knew that attacking merchant ships could be as effective a way of winning the War as throwing more men on to the battlefield.

Since 1916, the British Government had warned of the necessity of rationing if the War continued much longer. On 1 January 1917, the *South Wales Echo* reported on new regulations to enforce the adulteration of flour used to make bread with substitutes. The amount of sugar used in confectionery and mineral water was also drastically reduced, and milk was no longer to be used in making chocolate. The export of oats to Ireland was outlawed, in order to sustain supplies for the home market. Full scale rationing would come later, but even now in Cardiff and other cities across the United Kingdom, citizens were starting to experience shortages, with long queues forming outside shops.

The War had caused sharp increases in the price of beer and stout, and in April 1915 the manager of Cardiff's Brains Brewery wrote a letter to the *South Wales Echo* to explain the reasons behind the ever-increasing prices. At that time, mild beer was 6d a pint, while pale ale or stout cost 7d – a record high, the average pre-war price had been 3d for a pint of beer and 4d for stout. The brewery informed readers of the newspaper that prior to the War the company had produced around 36,000,000 standard barrels a year, but this had now dropped to 26,000,000. This had been compounded by the fact that, as of 1 April 1917, the food controller had suggested a further reduction in output to 18,200,000 barrels and the Government had prohibited the malting of barley, as it was to be reserved for the making of bread. The brewery argued that drinkers should accept these restrictions, as they were in the national interest, but that they regretted the necessary price increase. South Wales was not alone in seeing rising beer prices; the tax on beer had increased by nearly 250 per cent since 1914.

The biggest news to hit Cardiff in April 1917 was that America had now entered the War. The move was widely welcomed by the British public, and many felt that the support of the United States would make the already weakened German position almost untenable. This was, many believed, the beginning of the end of the War, which American involvement was bound to shorten. On 7 April, the *South Wales Echo* reproduced the text of a telegram sent by King George to the American President, thanking him for having brought America into the War:

> I desire on behalf of the Empire to offer my heartfelt congratulations to you on the entry of the United States of America into the war for the great ideals so nobly set forth in your speech to Congress.

America's first aggressive act was to seize the ninety-one German ships then docked in ports across the country. However, American involvement did not immediately solve all problems, and back in Britain the need for new recruits continued. Several more recruitment drives were held in Cardiff alone during 1917. Civilians were warned that many men were still avoiding conscription, and the term 'shirker' was by now the insult of the day. More raids were carried out by the military and local police across the area to identify so-called

Military advertisement (Note the strong-looking British soldier besting the German).

'shirkers'. Half a million more men were reportedly needed, and since the introduction of conscription the number of recruits had dropped to at least 100,000 below what was required.

Cardiff, like many other port cities, was facing the problem of caring for wounded soldiers, as casualties continued to arrive in the

The Royal Army Medical Corps march down Queen Street, Cardiff, in 1917.

city in huge numbers. The Cardiff Infirmary played a key role in caring for the war wounded, but it was never going to be able to accommodate the increasing numbers requiring beds. By mid-1917 several Cardiff schools had been transformed into hospitals. Often half of a school would remain open and the children would study in some of the classrooms, while injured soldiers were looked after in rooms nearby. The longer the War went on, the greater the need became for hospitals to care for the wounded, and soon convalescent soldiers wearing their distinctive blue dungarees, known as 'hospital blues', were a common sight on the streets of Cardiff.

CHAPTER 10

To Starve the Nation

For decades Britain had been dependent on imported foodstuffs and goods. The Germany military were only too aware of this fact and during the Great War they attempted to starve Britain into surrendering, using submarines to sink Allied merchant ships.

British merchant ships had first been targeted in 1914, but the attacks were ill-coordinated and by the beginning of 1915 the Germans had sunk only nineteen British ships. It was the introduction of unrestricted warfare that caused real problems for the British. German U-boat fleets were based in ports at Ostend and Bruges and could operate easily in the English Channel. Despite their small fleet of submarines, the Germans had spectacular results, sinking an average of 1.9 ships each day throughout the latter half of 1915. During this period, the Royal Navy were unable to detect enemy submarines and so U-boats could easily avoid patrolling British warships.

One method the Royal Navy used to combat the submarines was the reintroduction of the convoy system, which had been used effectively during the Napoleonic Wars to tackle French surface warships. Convoys now had strong naval escorts and from 1916 onwards these had great success in keeping up the flow of imported food to Britain and France. Aircraft were also used to protect merchant ships, alongside another method of protection known as 'dazzling'. This system, credited to the artist Norman Wilkinson, consisted of a series of geometric shapes in contrasting colours being painted on to the ships. This did not exactly conceal the ships, but made it difficult for the enemy to estimate their type, shape, size, speed and the direction in which they were heading. Over 2,000 ships were camouflaged using this method.

In late 1915, the British Admiralty offered £1,000 to the crew of any merchant ship who managed to sink an enemy submarine. The well-known industrialist Alfred Yarrow had also placed £20,000 with the Lloyd's Register so that amount could be doubled.

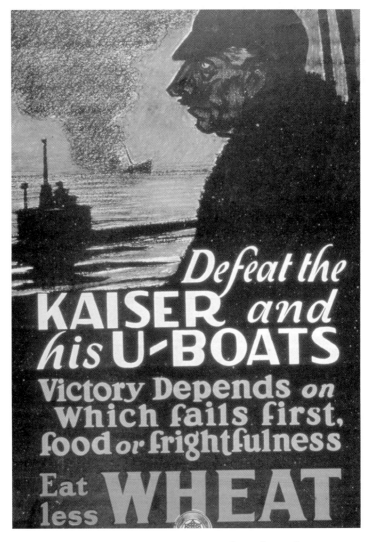

Government poster urging Britons to cut down their wheat consumption.

Smoke from the funnel was generally recognised as the first indication of the presence of a ship in the distance. Various ways of disguising the smoke were trialled, including spraying water over the funnel, which resulted in the escaping gas becoming heavier than air and descending, rather than drifting up into the sky. A device to create this effect was developed by Alfred Yarrow. It became known as the Yarrow Anti-submarine Smoke System and was fitted to many merchant ships. A number of merchant ships were also armed with guns, which were concealed and could be used to fire on any U-boats that came to the surface. Often U-boats would not use torpedoes to attempt to sink merchant ships, but would surface and fire their guns instead.

By 1917 the German U-boat attacks were sending huge quantities of food to the bottom of the sea and the resulting shortages had become a serious concern for the British Government. Propaganda was created, informing people to eat less, eat slower and from early 1918 many foods were rationed. Rationing helped to stabilise spiralling food prices which had caused great hardship, as some goods doubled or even quadrupled in cost, as with eggs.

Britain would not be starved into surrendering. A combination of rationing, naval convoys and home growing helped to feed households on the Home Front.

CHAPTER 11

1918 – Still No End in Sight

Timeline of key events in 1918

January

8   The American President Woodrow Wilson makes his 'Fourteen Points' statement. (This was the only statement of war aims issued by any of the nations involved in the conflict)

February

11   President Woodrow Wilson makes another speech to Congress, in which he establishes four principles to be upheld by American Forces during the War

March

21   Germany launches its spring offensive across several fronts. The offensive is designed to weaken British and French positions before American troops arrive in sufficient numbers to bolster the Allied positions

24   The British evacuate the town of Bapaume after intensive German shelling

26   An Allied Conference called by General Haig takes place in Doullens, in order to coordinate the Allied efforts along the Western Front

28   The German advance to the north of the Somme is halted by General Byng and the Third Army

April

1   The Royal Air Force is created by amalgamating the Royal
     Flying Corps and the Royal Naval Air Service
9   The German Army launches its second spring offensive and
     the Battle of Lys begins
12   General Haig issues his famous 'Backs to the Wall' order to
     British forces
23   The Royal Navy attempts to block the Belgian port of
     Zeebrugge, to prevent the Germans from using their U-boats
29   The German offensive in Flanders ends

May

9   The Royal Navy raids Ostend and HMS *Vindictive* is sunk,
     partially blocking the canal
27   The Third German spring offensive launches with the Third
     Battle of Aisne, which involves American forces for the first
     time
28   The American 28th Regiment of the 1st Division is victorious
     at Battle of Cantigny

June

6   American troops capture Bouresches
9   The Battle of Matz marks the fourth German offensive of the
     year

July

15   The Second Battle of the Marne sees yet another German
     offensive

August

6   The Second Battle of the Marne concludes with an Allied
     victory. This battle marks the start of the relentless Allied
     advance which continues until the Armistice. For this reason
     many consider it to be the battle that finally broke down the
     German Army

8   The Battle of Amiens begins, intended as the start of the
     Allied Hundred Days Offensive
26   The destruction of the German defences on the Hindenburg
     Line begins

September
3   German troops withdraw from Amiens to the Hindenburg Line
28   The final Allied advance on Flanders begins
29   The Germany Supreme Command informs the Kaiser that
     Germany's position is now hopeless

October
6   Germany seeks an armistice
11   Turkey requests an armistice
14   The Battle of Courtrai begins, ending with an Allied victory
21   Germany ceases unrestricted submarine warfare
23   British forces in Mesopotamia capture oil fields around Mosul

November
7   A German delegation crosses the Front Line in France to
     discuss surrender terms
9   Kaiser Wilhelm abdicates
11   The long awaited Armistice is agreed at 5.00am and become
     official at 11.00am, when the guns finally fall silent. At last
     the War ends

Nineteen-eighteen would finally see an end to the bloodshed, with a victory for the Allied forces, but as the year began few dared to believe that the conflict would be over within a matter of months. The mood of the nation was cautious as the New Year approached.

The *South Wales Echo* began 1918 with an apology to its readers for raising its cover price to one penny, due to ever-increasing production costs. Food shortages had also become a very real problem in the city, and Cardiff butchers had customers queuing outside their shops through the night, in order to be sure of being served when they opened. 'Bacon Queues', the *Western Mail* succinctly headed its report of the acute meat shortage. 'Many families in Cardiff will have to forego their Sunday joint this weekend,' the *Echo* stated.

> The shortage of meat of all kinds is very pronounced in the city and queues of poorly clad women and children can be seen outside butcher's shops throughout the city. The butchers being in the poor position of having little to offer customers and many of shops are closed; some are open only to regular customers.

The *Echo* went on to report that both Cardiff and Swansea markets were bare, and that there were shortages of goods such as butter, cheese and eggs. The supply of fresh fish into the city was also well below average and even where fish was available the prices were incredibly high. Sprats sold at 6d a pound and haddock was priced at 2d a pound, while kippers were costing 8d a pair. The price of fish, like that of many other foodstuffs, had more than doubled from pre-war prices.

While citizens were experiencing privations, they were also being asked to continue sending men to war. On 14 January, the *Western Mail* informed its readers that 45,000 more men were needed for the War Effort immediately. It warned that all industries not essential to the War would suffer, as more and more men were conscripted into uniform. The War, it seemed, was turning into a never-ending cycle.

The next day, there were incredible scenes in the Valleys town of Bargoed, when hundreds of people arrived by train and congregated outside multiple shops in the town. There were queues for margarine and tea, with frantic rushes from one shop to another as they opened. Order was successfully maintained by the local police force and incredibly no damage was done. In the evening a noisy 400-strong crowd of men and women marched into Gilfach Bargoed, intending to discover if there were any food stocks available in the shops there. From Gilfach Bargoed, the crowd moved on to Pengam and Fleur-de-lis and demanded that shopkeepers produce any stock they had left. The shopkeepers allowed their premises to be inspected and when no hidden stockpiles were discovered the crowd dispersed peacefully.

The same day, there was also a disturbance in the Rhondda Valleys which became a near-riot, when some 3,000 people gathered outside the New Market Stores in Tonypandy. The stores were closed and people started kicking the doors, as the crowds shouted to be allowed in to inspect the food stocks. The police arrived and endeavoured to pacify the crowd. In the end, Inspector James Davies entered the shop and, after he had examined the supply of butter, told the gathered crowd there were insufficient supplies for even the store's registered customers. After this point the crowd dispersed without further incident. Shops were also besieged in Tonyrefail, Gilfach Goch and Merthyr, but always with the same result: none had been hoarding food.

Scenes like these were played out all over the United Kingdom, and it came as no surprise when the Government announced the introduction of food rationing. At a meeting in Tonypandy on 17 January 1918 representatives from the Food Control Committee informed residents that food supplies would be carefully controlled, so that local people would get a fair share of whatever was available. There were constant interruptions from local women during the meeting, and the executive officer of the committee sternly advised the crowd that the cooperation of the public was essential during these troubled times. One local storekeeper, a Mr Bowen, stated before the meeting that during the previous day he had sold 300 pots of jam within an hour and that he had found it necessary to pack food in secret at his warehouse, for fear of burglaries. The meeting ended with a resolution to request the Government to introduce compulsory food rationing.

On the same day, the *South Wales Echo* reported huge queues in Cardiff, with the Hayes shopping area seeing the greatest numbers. The journalist noted the 'pitiful condition' of some of the older women as they queued in the snow and rain to obtain a little butter or margarine. Police were again on hand to control the large crowds, and in some cases had to help shopkeepers to distribute the meagre supplies they had.

'Long, Long Queues', the *South Wales Echo* reported on 18 January:

There were queues of all sorts and sizes in the city today – queues for butter, margarine, bacon and other meats. The one

Food queues became a regular sight on the streets of Cardiff.

thing all of the queues had in common is that they were mostly made up of women. They waited patiently in the rain, the snow beneath their feet turned into slush while the policemen on duty shepherded them like sheep from shop to shop.

The police presence was proved useful on occasions. During one incident, a constable stopped a woman, noticing that she had already been into the same shop that day. When her bag was searched it was discovered that she had three times the half-pound amount of butter being served, and had already been served three times before attempting to obtain a fourth portion. It was also reported that a certain Cardiff shopkeeper had hoarded a tray of butter for so long that it had gone bad. The newspaper concluded that such scenes made a persuasive argument for a national food rationing scheme to be introduced. As with conscription previously, there was a reluctance to introduce nationwide food rationing, but the situation was becoming so dire that the Government had no alternative.

The food shortages continued, and soon serious disorder began to seem likely. On 21 January, shop windows were smashed in the Valleys town of Maerdy because it was rumoured that food was being hoarded inside. The rumours proved to be false, but police had to be drafted in from other towns to restore order. There were similar scenes across the Valleys, and in the market town of Pontypridd a butcher was knocked unconscious by an unknown assailant, as he tried to close his shop. Local councils started to introduce schemes whereby food would only be sold to local residents, in an attempt to reduce hoarding.

In February 1918, national food rationing was finally introduced, with ration books issued to the entire British population by local food committees. The Ministry of Food adjusted supplies on a week-by-week basis. On 7 February, the Ministry of Food extended the powers of the local food committees, allowing them to control the sale of all foodstuffs. The committees now held a great deal of power over shops and were able to take charge of distribution.

Some issues continued to be debated, such as one suggestion intended to alleviate the meat shortage, that horseflesh be sold in markets. Perhaps unsurprisingly, the theft of sheep from the Welsh mountains became a real problem and there were livestock thefts at many of the farms around Cardiff, as well as much further afield.

There were occasionally a few more light-hearted incidents involving hoarding. On 7 April 1918, the *Glamorgan Gazette* reported the story of two schoolboys who had been exploring the caves in Cymparc in the Rhondda Valleys, when they discovered a box in one of the caverns containing oleaginous matter wrapped in paper. The boys were terrified, thinking the strange objects may be some kind of German explosive, and they reported their mysterious find to the local police. When, it was investigated, the police discovered that the box contained around 20lbs of butter which someone had obviously been hiding. All the previous week schoolteachers had been visiting homes

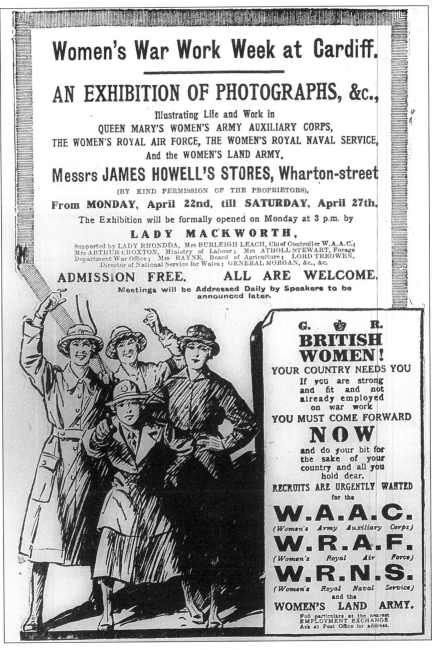

Patriotism played a heavy part in the push to get women into war work.

in the area to ensure there was no food hoarding going on, and they realised that someone had hidden the butter to conceal it from the authorities.

Coal rationing had been commonplace in London for more than a year by 1918, and now these measures were rolled out across the nation. It was now against the law to cook food in any public establishment, including restaurants, hotels and inns, between the hours of 9.30pm and 5.00am. 'No hot meals after 9.30pm to ensure we win the war,' the *South Wales Echo* warned in an article on the latest restrictions. All places of amusement were to be closed by 10.30pm and not reopened before 1.00pm the following day. Coal supplies were heavily restricted for both businesses and private dwellings.

Despite the increasing restrictions, the War Effort continued. On 22 April, 'Women's War Work Week' began in Cardiff, intended to urge more women to volunteer or join one of the women's services. An exhibition was to be held at the Howell's store on Wharton Street, involving guest speakers and displays designed to show the many opportunities for women to take part in the War Effort. This was seen as essential at the stage in the conflict, especially as from 25 April 1918 men up to the age of fifty would be called up. Men were informed that strict medical examinations would be carried out before they were drafted, and that armed combat would be unlikely. Most of the men in this upper age group would serve as war workers or in the Home Guard.

The idea that the end of the War might be only months away was something few would have considered at a time when the effects of long years of war were really starting to bite on the Home Front. This was compounded by industrial unrest. In May 1918, 800 men from the Cardiff Corporation, all members of the Municipal Employees Association, came out on strike. It was reported in the *South Wales Echo* that the city's lamplighters, gardeners, scavengers, and roadmen were all preparing to strike, along with the entire staff of Cardiff Cemetery and most of the cleaners at Cardiff's City Hall. The reason for the strike was that the Association was demanding an advance on wages for Cardiff workers to bring them into line with other corporations nationwide. Cardiff's Lord Mayor was forced to make a request in the *South Wales Echo* for volunteer gravediggers, after health concerns were raised over bodies remaining unburied.

There seemed to be more to celebrate at the Front, however, as newspaper headlines announced one Allied victory after another. 'German Withdrawal', the *South Wales Echo* stated in the morning edition of 16 August 1918. The related article reported that the British had crossed the Ancre. The following Monday, the newspaper claimed that the Allies had had a great weekend and were galloping over the enemy. 'The Greatest British Victory of the War,' the *Echo* claimed, when Welsh troops retook Mametz Wood – the same area where the Cardiff City Battalion had suffered such huge losses in 1916.

'Enemy falling back on large front,' the *Echo* suggested on 3 September, stating that '10,000 prisoners were taken yesterday'. The Germans were now said to be in an impossible position, and there was a feeling that the War would not continue for long. It was hard for many to imagine after so many years of deadly conflict, that soon the guns would indeed fall silent.

On 3 October the headlines uniformly reported that German forces had begun to retreat in Flanders. Prior to the War this area that had been unknown by most British people, but it was now almost symbolic of the trench warfare on the Western Front, which had dominated the War for so long. If the Germans were leaving Flanders then surely it was only a matter of time until an end to the fighting was reached.

On 10 October, the *South Wales Echo* carried a story headlined, 'The Kaiser Reported Abdication':

A rumour which started in Berlin, and has now spread all over Germany, is characteristic of the present state of mind of the people which allows them to believe something that only weeks ago would have been dangerous even to whisper about. The rumour is to the effect that the Kaiser intends to abdicate in favour of his eldest grandson, Prince Wilhelm. So widespread is the rumour that Berlin has been moved to make a denial.

The newspaper also took great pride in reporting that former Lord Mayor of Cardiff, R. J. Smith, had recently joined up and would serve in the Medical Corps.

The *South Wales Echo* revealed on 30 October, that a total of 30,000 German prisoners of war were being held on the Somme and that 500 guns had also been taken. The following day saw the sensational news that Turkey had surrendered, and the day after Austria followed, but still the German Army held out. German leaders were involved in frantic negations with the Allies, attempting to obtain more favourable conditions before agreeing to an armistice. The War continued meanwhile, with new names added to the casualty lists every day.

Finally, on 11 November 1918, the *South Wales Echo* carried the long awaited headline: 'Germany surrendered this morning!' The Great War was over. This conflict had initially been seen as a glorious adventure, only for the realisation to set in that this would be

Cardiff's former Lord Mayor R. J. Smith.

remembered as a terrible period in human history. It was a time of innovation in the art of warfare and a time when the human race demonstrably attained the ability to destroy itself. It was to be described as a war so terrible, so brutal and so costly that it that it would end all wars. If only that were true.

CHAPTER 12

We Will Never Forget Them: Local War Memorials

They shall grow not old, as we that are left grow old:
Age shall not weary them, nor the years condemn.
At the going down of the sun and in the morning
We will remember them.

(Extract from 'Fallen' by Laurence Binyon,
published in *The Times*, 21 September 1914.)

Llandaff War Memorial.

Pontyclun War Memorial.

*Cowbridge
War Memorial.*

Tonyrefail War Memorial.

Miskin War Memorial.

*Llandaff Cathedral School
War Memorial.*

Porth War Memorial.

1914 – 1918

LIEUT JAMES C. WILLIAMS
17TH R.W.F.
SEC. LIEUT JACK EVANS
COLDSTREAM. GDS.
CORPL WILLIAM J. JONES
4TH BATT. S.W.B.
DRIVR EDWARD BROWN
R.F.A. 28TH DIV.
" " HENRY FARNHAM
R.F.A. 38TH DIV.
GUNR SIDNEY WORGAN
R.G.A.
PTE. DAVID WORGAN
18TH CLOSTERS
" CHARLES WORGAN
18TH CLOSTERS
" WILLIAM COTTRELL
S.W.B.
" CHARLES COTTRELL
2ND WELSH REG.
" REGINALD SHEPPARD
17TH WELSH REG.
" ERNEST BEAVINGTON
14TH HUSSARS
" GEORGE MERRY
2ND MTN.REG.
" FRANCIS COLES
RIFLE BRGDE. WELSH REG.
" HENRY LEWIS
S.W.B.
" GEORGE WILLIAMS

" THOMAS W. WYATT
R.F.
SERGT RICHARD SMITH
2ND WELSH REG.

CPL LIONEL HY LANDEG
15TH WORCESTERS
PTE. THOMAS E. WORGAN
2ND BATT. B.O.Y.L.I.

AFGHANISTAN WAR
GDSMN. CRAIG ANDREW RODERICK
1ST BATT. WELSH GUARDS
GDSMN. JAMIE SHADRAKE
1ST BATT. GRENADIER GUARDS

Llanharan War Memorial.

THE following account appeared in the Battalion Orders of the 11th Battalion Welsh Regiment.

" The Commanding Officer wishes to place on record his appreciation of the magnificent work done by the Battalion on the nights of the 22nd and 23rd October, 1916. The raiding party were admirably assisted by some R.E. and extra regimental stretcher bearers. The Battalion had to carry out a long and dangerous advance before reaching their position of deployment. The silent manner in which this was carried out was proved by the fact that the party was able to go most of the way without a single enemy shot being fired. The remainder of the advance which had to be carried out under a heavy fire of every description is a striking tribute to the coolness and courage of the men.

The storming of the enemy's trenches, in the face of a stubborn resistance.

The raiding of enemy dug-outs.

The defeat of enemy counter attack, and

The capture of prisoners were worthy of the highest praise.

The withdrawal from the enemy's trenches and return to our lines under intense barrage called for high qualities of courage and steadiness. Both flank-guards to whom were entrusted the important work of guarding the flanks, carried out these duties in the most admirable manner. Though mourning the death of three of our comrades it is gratifying to know that our casualties were very slight. No troops could have behaved with greater gallantry and dash, and the operations throughout will add another page to the glorious history of the Welch Regt."

Cardiff Pals battle orders.

Select Bibliography

NEWSPAPERS
Western Mail
South Wales Echo
Rhondda Leader
Pontypridd Observer
Glamorgan Gazette

ARCHIVES
Private Papers
The National Archives
The Royal British Legion

WEBSITES
Memories of World War 1 –
http://memoriesofworldwarone.blogspot.co.uk
Rhondda Remembers – www.rhonddaremembers.com
BBC History – www.bbc.co.uk/history/0/ww1
Project Gutenberg – www.gutenberg.org
Wales Online – www.walesonline.co.uk/all-about/first-world-war

BOOKS
I am indebted to all those who have written on the Great War and found many books invaluable in my research for this work. Among those I frequently revisited were:

The Oxford History of the First World War (Oxford University Press, 1998)

Max Arthur, *The Last Post* (Orion Books, 2005)

K Cooper and J. E. Davies, *The Welsh Regiment* (Militaria Cymraeg, 1998)

Max Hastings, *Catastrophe* (William Collins, 2014)

Jeremy Paxman, *Great Britain's Great War* (Penguin, 2014)

Hew Strachan, *The First World War* (Simon and Schuster, 2003)

Index